"He pro. won't shoot you"

"He probably won't shoot you"

Memoir of an Adult Protective Services Case Manager

MARK MEHLER

Foreword by Kathleen Quinn

McFarland & Company, Inc., Publishers
Jefferson, North Carolina

LIBRARY OF CONGRESS CATALOGUING-IN-PUBLICATION DATA

Names: Mehler, Mark, 1948– author.
Title: "He probably won't shoot you" : memoir of an adult protective
services case manager / Mark Mehler ; foreword by Kathleen Quinn.
Description: Jefferson, North Carolina : McFarland & Company, Inc., 2021 |
Includes index.
Identifiers: LCCN 2021010607 | ISBN 9781476682341 (paperback: acid free paper) ∞
ISBN 9781476643687 (ebook)
Subjects: LCSH: Mehler, Mark, 1948– | Social workers—United
States—Biography. | Older people—Care—United States. | People with
disabilities—Care—United States. | BISAC: SOCIAL SCIENCE / Human
Services
Classification: LCC HV40.32.M44 A3 2021 | DDC 362.6/8253092 [B]—dc23
LC record available at https://lccn.loc.gov/2021010607

BRITISH LIBRARY CATALOGUING DATA ARE AVAILABLE

ISBN (print) 978-1-4766-8234-1
ISBN (ebook) 978-1-4766-4368-7

Front cover image © Pavel Kubarkov/Shutterstock

Printed in the United States of America

*McFarland & Company, Inc., Publishers
Box 611, Jefferson, North Carolina 28640
www.mcfarlandpub.com*

Table of Contents

Table of Contents

Foreword

BY KATHLEEN QUINN

Former president of the National APS Association in Washington, D.C.

Every community, in fact every neighborhood in this country, has within it older people and disabled adults who are being mistreated by others or cannot meet their most basic needs for health and safety (self-neglect). These are our most vulnerable citizens, and they often suffer for years, while remaining largely invisible to the greater world.

Adult Protective Services (APS) is likewise largely unknown and unrecognized, yet it's the social service system charged with responding to reports of mistreatment of vulnerable adults and investigating cases of suspected abuse, neglect, financial exploitation, and self-neglect. In so doing, APS makes every attempt to protect these victims while preserving their rights to autonomy and self-direction.

Mark Mehler's memoir is, to my knowledge, the first nonfiction book to ever look at APS from the inside. It describes the daily challenges of working to protect adults who cannot protect themselves. This work is frequently dangerous and extremely frustrating. Perpetrators, most often family members, may be impaired themselves, or they may be utterly greedy and selfish people using their elderly relatives for their own ends.

This book will open the eyes of readers to the fascinating, sad, occasionally funny, sometimes sordid, and often tragic world of elder and vulnerable adult abuse. Mark Mehler has a gift for storytelling, and he makes these pages come alive with real-world situations that may seem at first unbelievable but are all too real and all too common. Although set in New York City, the clients described herein could be found anywhere in America.

And while the New York City services described are similar to those of most APS programs around the country, program eligibility requirements, training, timelines, and resources vary significantly from state to state, and even from county to county. This is because, until the last few years, there has been no sustained federal attention given to APS, and to this day, vulnerable adult victims of abuse, neglect, and exploitation get no designated funding for protective services. As pointed out in the book, one study found that funding for child victims was estimated at $45 per client versus less than $4 per adult victim.

While excellent books have been written about elder abuse, they are by and large scholarly in nature, providing the most up-to-date research and data on the many aspects of this complex and vexing issue. In contrast, *He Probably Won't Shoot You,* based on Mark's seven years as an APS case manager, presents the hands-on, day-to-day experiences of field workers, the clients, and their families. It explores the difficulties involved in negotiating the social, healthcare, criminal justice, and other bureaucratic systems that exist to help these victims. Those negotiations can be delicate and harrowing.

You will come away from this book with an appreciation for the complexity and difficulty of protecting vulnerable adults, and a greater understanding of how the all-encompassing issues of healthcare, client safety, financial security, crime, housing, and public health intersect with an adult's right to self-determination. And, you will come away with one more thing: an appreciation for the dedication and untiring work of legions of APS investigators and case managers throughout the land.

As a 30-year veteran of APS work at both the state and national levels, I have been incredibly frustrated at the lack of recognition, respect, and resources accorded to Adult Protective Services. It is well past time that the extraordinary efforts of APS workers are supported by local and state governments, and, most of all, by our federal government.

I sincerely hope this book will help bring some of that long-overdue appreciation for the needs—and the value—of these vulnerable adult lives, and for the people dedicated to protecting them.

After serving for 10 years as the executive director of the National Adult Protective Services Association (NAPSA), Kathleen Quinn retired in August 2016. She then went on to serve as the president of the NAPSA board from 2019 to 2020. Prior to her work at NAPSA, she served as the seniors advisor to the Illinois Attorney General, was the APS administrator in Illinois for 15 years, and helped to build the domestic violence network in Illinois.

Introduction:
Happiness Is No Gun

A hero is somebody who voluntarily walks into the unknown.
—Tom Hanks

The client was an 80-ish Chinese American woman living in a cluttered apartment in Flushing, Queens. According to the referral from a hospital social worker, she was undergoing regular beatings from her son, a New York City police officer.

I had been trying to contact the referral source (RS) for additional information and clarification, but as New York City Adult Protective Services' regulations mandate an initial home visit (IHV) within 72 hours of receipt of the referral, I had no choice but to venture forth without benefit of all the facts.

Only steps from the client's building, the RS rang up my cell. I expressed to her my discomfort at the prospect of confronting an alleged perpetrator wielding a 9mm Glock.

"Oh, I wouldn't worry too much about that," said the RS, in her most reassuring social worker voice. "He probably won't shoot you."

"That's very comforting," I replied, oozing sarcasm.

No. That's what, in hindsight, I wished I had replied.

What I do recall saying was something along the lines of, "Uh, okay.... Thanks."

I rode the elevator to the client's apartment and knocked gently on her door (while standing off to the side to dodge the bullets). The client, a frail, white-haired lady with papery skin, dressed in bedclothes and looking about as old as old can look, slowly opened the door a crack and beckoned me inside. Reluctantly, and with the aforementioned misgivings, I slipped through the door and into the breach....

As any veteran Adult Protective Services case manager will tell you, one of the first rules of APS work cannot be found in any official training manual. The acronym for this is "NBR," which stands for Never Believe the Referral.

This case was a poster-child for NBR. As it turns out, the client, a hoarder of old clothes and cardboard boxes was a very nervous lady and also a harridan of the first magnitude. Her son, a thoroughly decent but hapless chap, had all he could do to simultaneously assist his anxiety-ridden mother and maintain his own tenuous hold on sanity. Not a healthy situation for one of New York's Finest.

After a couple of grueling hours spent refereeing these two, it was only my pacifist leanings and what was left of my professionalism that kept me from advising the officer to take out his service weapon and use it in a good cause.

However, another rule of thumb in the APS business states that one cannot accurately gauge the progress, let alone the outcome, of a case based on one harrowing home visit. This case actually had a favorable conclusion. The presence of an outsider, over time, seemed to relax the client and help her get to that emotional place where she could finally accept support from a social service agency, and even from her beleaguered, yet still caring, son.

APS ultimately conducted a heavy-duty cleaning of her apartment and assisted the client with a referral for much-needed couple's therapy for mother and child. The last time I saw her, she was enjoying living in a cleaner and saner environment. In the end, I have to say I am very glad that her son, the cop, kept his gun holstered. Chalk this one up on the plus side.

The following memoir is a look back on my seven-year journey in the adult protection trade. In it, I hope not only to reveal a world that very few people see (and many may not wish to see), but to address, through my own on-the-job experience, why and how people do this work, what they take away from it, and the price they pay to do it.

It has been nearly a decade since I retired from APS crisis management, and I'm only now realizing just how extraordinary a thing it is to walk into someone's life—most often one characterized by financial and spiritual poverty and excruciating emotional pain—at a moment in time when that already-tattered life has been turned upside-down. Be it the threat of homelessness, lack of food, needed medical or psychiatric treatment, or unspeakable cruelty inflicted by a loved one, you've just walked into a lion's den of dysfunction. Because this is a mandated rather than a traditional voluntary social service, you are stuck there, searching for what seems like another desperate solution to an intractable problem.

Making the whole experience even more extraordinary is how very often the APS crisis worker, at the moment of introduction, represents the only person in the client's life who cares at all whether he or she lives or dies. In these instances, the worker, if so inclined, can take on a secondary, but more profound role: that of a *witness.*

All of us, in our daily lives, bear witness to one another. We are each other's memory keepers, storehouses of all our joys and pains. Through the sharing of our stories, having them heard and accepted, our brief lives can transcend time. It follows, then, that bearing witness to people at their lowest, most vulnerable and most disaffected moments, is among the highest of human callings.

I think about all this now, but I didn't very much back then. I was much too busy trying to stay abreast of the daily ebb and flow of my caseload, trying to keep calamity at bay. But, in retrospect, I would like to think that even in the absence of a solution, or even the right words to say, I was still on the scene, bearing witness.

Tolstoy famously wrote that happy families are all alike, while each unhappy one is unhappy in its own way. Sometimes I wonder if Tolstoy, or someone he knew, worked a stint at Moscow APS. All the clients described in this book are, indeed, unhappy in their own fashions. Many of their cases are heartbreakingly sad, tragic, or tragi-comic. Others are strange and/or profoundly weird. Some are magically uplifting, and they are the ones that keep you coming back for more, despite all the frustrations and the lack of anything remotely approaching a living wage.

And more than a few cases, I say with some regret, are out-and-out disgusting, which is why my wife, who is not the squeamish type, insisted on hearing about my day at least an hour after we had finished dinner. And even then, it could be touch-and-go. For the faint of stomach, I have trod carefully, and euphemistically, in describing the very worst of these situations.

Many of the cases cited in this book were assigned to me back in the day. I played a backup role in others that were formally assigned to colleagues. And some were cases I heard about after work, winding down in a local bar with a cool bourbon and a weary smile.

It's all a rich tapestry.

None of the clients referenced in the book is identified by name, and nearly all the case managers and other professionals have likewise

Introduction

had their names changed or have requested that their comments be unattributed. In a number of cases, I've fudged some insignificant details (for example, changing a Brooklyn case to a Queens locale). All these minor alterations have been made to more fully adhere to the ethical imperative of strict client confidentiality.

Fortunately, my long-term memory remains sturdy and authoritative—just last week, off the top of my head, I was able to rattle off 91 of the 93 winners of the Oscar for Best Actor in a Leading Role (apologies to Eddie Redmayne and Rami Malek). Still, nearly all the events chronicled here occurred 10 to 15 years ago, making it necessary to reach out to colleagues familiar with my old cases to help fill some of the gaps in my memory. All told, I did my best to color in the details, gory and otherwise.

Moreover, as I was not taking a reporter's copious notes during my APS home visits, all dialogue from that period is an approximation. However, it's one that I believe accurately portrays the tenor of those long-ago conversations. Interviews conducted with sources in the here and now are verbatim, or reasonably close to it.

I should further advise you that there will be times, as you're reading this book, when you will put it aside and say to yourself that the writer has clearly allowed his over-active imagination to run wild on the printed page. And I wouldn't fault you in the least for thinking that way.

All I can do is assure you that, for all intents and purposes, the stories contained herein are true, and offer my suggestion that you never underestimate the propensity of human beings to behave outlandishly.

Furthermore, I apologize in advance if in the telling of these tales, I come off as irreverent, flippant, jaundiced, or casually bemused. Like laughter, these are endemic in APS work, and essential defenses against a daily immersion in human misery.

Of all the APS foot soldiers mentioned in this volume, a few are still out there on the streets, fighting the good fight to keep very bad things from becoming much worse things. Most have since moved on to less stressful pursuits or into retirement, but they still carry a little APS with them wherever they go.

As I write this, during the first terrifying and despairing months of a global coronavirus pandemic, my own days at APS feel almost idyllic. While the basics of the job itself, and the dynamics of human dysfunction, do not change all that much from year to year, today's Adult Protective Services crisis managers are operating in a new and highly charged arena. In New York, they are now viewed as part of that vast army of "essential workers," tasked with keeping the nation afloat while it waits with bated breath for a miracle cure or vaccine.

It is one thing to help keep a fellow human being safe in his or her home; it is a much more burdensome thing to do it from at least six feet away, gloved, masked, goggled, and scared half to death. Some APS workers are receiving "hero pay." Not that this brings their remuneration to a level that's proportional to their efforts and their sacrifice, but it helps, nonetheless.

To all these courageous workers throughout the land, many of them from the much-derided Millennial Generation, as well as those who blazed the trail before them and the supervisors who have had their backs, this book is fondly dedicated.

CHAPTER 1

Welcome to Countertransference

I have an APS dream.

It's my only such dream, and it's been recurring for more than 10 years, ever since I retired from full-time crisis management. Fortunately, it recurs infrequently—every 8 or 10 months or so. In the dream, I have a problem client, an old lady closely resembling actress Margaret Hamilton (a.k.a. the Wicked Witch of the West), who resides in a dilapidated, multi-family wooden shack in lower Manhattan. I have not visited her in months. But every morning, I come into the office, pick her thin file out of a metal cabinet, skim its contents, and tell myself that today is the day I'm finally going to make that visit. I'm consumed with guilt for not doing anything to assist this poor woman with the dark eyes and sharp nose, and I'm equally concerned that my bosses will one day take a look at the file and start asking probing questions for which I have no answers. But, for whatever reason, I'm unable to hoist myself out of my chair and make that long-overdue home visit. I wake from this nightmare wishing to banish it from memory with the greatest alacrity.

Anyway, I kept the dream to myself for years. Just recently, I sought out the counsel of my wife, who is a psychotherapist by profession and generally loath to cross that dangerous divide between spouse and shrink.

I gave her the particulars of my persistent dreamscape, including the fact that I am not always fully dressed and the not insignificant detail that, as a small child, I was terrified by the Wicked Witch's fearsome army of flying monkeys. I told her of my lingering regret at not telling Ms. Hamilton about this when the two of us chanced to share a hospital elevator back in the early 1980s. By that time, the actress had become even more famous as a pitchperson for Maxwell House Coffee.

"All right," the wife sighed. "Can we just for the moment put aside Margaret and her vicious monkeys and focus on the core of the dream, which is very clear. It's all about you and your entire APS experience. It speaks to all those people you couldn't help, and all those things you wished you could do for them but couldn't."

Knowing me as well as she does, my wife continued with her whistle-stop analysis.

"This is a job that demands that you're able to maintain a certain separation between your professional duties and your personal life. For you, the clients were, to a large degree, proxies for the family you couldn't heal. That may be one major reason you got into this work in the first place, and why in your dream life, you're still conflating your own family with your APS quasi-family."

"Maybe," she concluded, combining the best of a psychotherapist's guidance and a wife's deep caring, "this is something you might want to work on therapeutically going forward."

Indeed, it might well be. Maybe, in some way, that's what I'm doing writing this memoir.

I arrived at Adult Protective Services in March 2004, via a circuitous path. Apart from the above-mentioned human impulse, there were other feelings that led me there. I'll deal with the most logical ones first. I will try not to come off in the telling as a fourth-rate Charles Dickens.

My first 32 years of working life were spent as a writer and editor for newspapers, magazines, and vampire corporations. They were pretty good years, taking me to more than 20 countries around the world, earning me some decent money and bolstering an occasionally fragile ego with a byline. Nevertheless, there came a point where it dawned on me that a lot of what I had been writing was directed primarily toward making exceedingly rich people even richer.

By the late 1990s, I had begun thinking heavily along more altruistic lines. Maybe it was time to start giving back, I thought. Hard work, combined with frugality and good fortune (a family inheritance, savvy investing, and a couple of stock option windfalls) gave me the financial freedom to consider migrating down into a less rarified income tax bracket.

The events of 9/11/2001 brought these deliberations to a much higher level. The magazine I was working on at the time went belly-up not long after the Twin Towers came tumbling down. The president of the United States, for his part, was calling on patriotic Americans to go shopping, but I've always abhorred all forms of shopping, with the sole exception of antiquing. Instead, I chose to heed the call of a sermon I heard a rabbi give in the weeks following the attack.

"The only thing one can do in response to this kind of unspeakable tragedy," intoned the rabbi, "is to be *better*. Commit, today, to becoming a better person, a better parent, a better spouse, a better neighbor."

I'd heard this particular rabbi give many sermons over the years, but I can't recall being greatly moved by any of them. I left the synagogue on that Sabbath eve thinking that this elderly rabbi would do well to retire immediately, as he'd never be able to top this sermonic swan song.

As the rabbi had so eloquently suggested, I walked out resolved to commit myself to toiling in the service of the public good and welfare.

I spent most of 2002 doing some freelance writing, substitute teaching at a charter elementary school in Queens, and taking a course to become an Emergency Medical Technician. I got a job with a for-profit ambulance service, lasting in that position for four whole days.

I recall transporting to a hospital a severely disabled youngster whose uncle was a former college basketball player I had once interviewed as a sports reporter. I was enjoying talking to the kid about his uncle and hopefully taking a small piece of his mind off his intense back pain. The senior ambulance supervisor took me aside and told me in no uncertain terms that a good bedside manner would get me nowhere on this job.

This was not the kind of altruism I wanted to practice.

Very shortly thereafter, with the assistance of my wife, I landed a part-time job with a Project Liberty team. Project Liberty was the federal boondoggle passed in the wake of 9/11 to assist victims with counseling and other social services. I say "boondoggle" because I was a personal witness to thousands of wasted taxpayer dollars.

My job on the team was running seminars on post-traumatic stress and anger management at senior centers, churches, and other places where anxious seniors congregate. I got pretty good at taking old people to their "special places."

When the federal trough finally ran dry in the summer of 2003, I got my first full-time social services job with a non-profit agency that sent people out into the field to counsel victims of elder abuse and educate law enforcement officers and other public servers-and-protectors about how to recognize EA in their communities. I especially liked talking to the cops at morning roll call. Most of them were eager for this information, and they asked good, thoughtful questions.

The client aspect of the work was not as rewarding. I had virtually no on-the-job supervision, and with a caseload of 35 or more, I was in way over my head and forced to rely on common sense (not always my strong suit).

I particularly recollect one client who had to sneak out of her house once a week to visit with me in a diner. She and her aged husband had been held for years as prisoners in their home by their mentally ill son. I never got to meet the son but I imagined him as a strapping 30-something with a horrifying mixture of diabolical intent (think Charles Boyer in "Gaslight") and schizophrenia.

One of his most dastardly methods of psychological torment was to barge unannounced and uninvited into his parents' bedroom during baseball season and awaken them to the sound of his play-by-play recap of the entire evening's Mets game. To the average New Yorker, about the only thing worse than hearing a lengthy recap of a Mets game is having it delivered by a large, threatening schizophrenic who refuses to take no for an answer.

My wife had told me about a technique called "cognitive behavioral therapy," which focuses on the problem at hand and finding effective strategies to address identified client goals. This was accomplished via baby steps aimed at gradually freeing the client and her husband—who suffered from congestive heart failure aggravated by the nightly Mets commentary—from the son's tyrannical control.

My initial suggestion was to simply put a lock on the bedroom door and see what happened. The client followed my advice and told me at our next meeting that after banging on the door for a half-hour, her son went quietly back to his room to deliver his nightly Mets recap into his pillow.

A small victory, to be sure, but an important one. The game was on.

My next brilliant suggestion was that his mother stop doing his laundry. The client tried it out on the son, and it worked, as well. Then, she took it still further and stopped cooking three meals a day for him.

And, with one small behavioral triumph after another, it became clear that she and her ailing husband had thoroughly committed to unleashing themselves from the shackles of warped parenthood.

The final step in the process called for the couple to take a vacation, something they had not done since the Carter administration. The son initially took very poorly to this idea, but, again, after loud theatrics and empty threats, the young man caved, and Mr. and Mrs. X went to stay with Mrs. X's cousin in Pennsylvania for an entire week.

Mrs. X was virtually a new woman when she returned, and she expressed her gratitude for having helped steer the couple toward a healthier and more independent life. I would have liked to have seen this case through to a conclusion, except that unexpected events intervened.

I walked into the office one morning in February 2004 and found the place crawling with agents from the New York City Department of Investigation. They were going through records and grilling staff members. It was not a good look for any agency. I'll spare you the unpleasant details, but there was some ongoing financial hanky-panky taking place in one of the organization's major capital spending projects. The criminal investigation had nothing to do with the case management unit of which I was a part.

Nevertheless, the scene that morning unsettled me just a bit, and while the DOI was rummaging, stone-faced, through the files, I phoned up an old buddy of mine, a criminal defense lawyer.

"I don't think this is anything to worry about," I told him, "but the fuzz is buzzing all around me, and they don't look at all happy."

"Okay," my would-be attorney said. "You have only one job now and that is to shut the f—k up. Don't even give them your name. If they start pressing you, call me back, and I'll come over there."

Days later, the agency lost its government funding and on a subsequent Friday afternoon, around closing time, management told us not to bother showing up for work on Monday if we were interested in getting paid past today. In true altruistic fashion, I returned to a pay-free environment on Monday morning and managed to close or refer out all my cases over the next 48 hours.

I wasn't worried, as I had a good line on a job with another New York City non-profit, this one contracted to provide Adult Protective Services. I was about to experience March Madness in a whole new way.

The APS job interview was my first-ever "group interview," featuring myself, two younger female applicants—an African American and a Russian émigré, both capable and qualified—the program director, and a supervisor. It was all quite pleasant. I thought I came off okay for someone with limited field experience and of advanced age. I impressed the supervisor with the maturity and wisdom that often accompanies 56 years of daily living, as well as my interviewing skills gleaned from three decades of news and feature reporting.

"He probably won't shoot you"

The program director was less impressed and preferred to hire someone younger, someone with more experience who needed the job more and was possessed of greater stamina. His reticence, as I came to find out, was understandable. He had had quite enough of the newly hired reporting for work on Monday, getting an initial whiff of life in the APS hothouse, and scampering off before receiving the first weekly paycheck.

"The first days are the hardest days," wrote Jerome J. Garcia of the Grateful Dead. To many fledgling APS workers, they are intolerable days.

"For my first six months, I struggled with my conscience every morning about whether to come into work at all," relates a former colleague. "Truthfully, I wouldn't have made it through the first week without strong support at home and a great team in the office."

The boss feared I could turn out to be one of those "snowflakes" just flitting by on the way to a normal job.

But the supervisor remained insistent. This is the guy you should hire, she kept telling the boss. Trust me, he won't let you down. Ultimately, despite his lingering doubts, the director succumbed to her entreaties and brought me onboard for a try-out.

On my first day on the job, I was in his office getting an initial, de facto orientation, when a co-worker busted in like the Mad Hatter on acid.

"I did it!" she screamed. "I got in!"

"That's wonderful," said the boss. "That's great work."

It took her a minute or so to calm down. For weeks, she had been attempting every crisis management trick to gain access to a client's home in order to perform her initial assessment. Gaining the trust of a client to let you into his or her home may not seem like a major breakthrough, and in other social services contexts, it isn't. But at APS, just getting all the way through the door that first time can be a huge accomplishment.

Still, having spent less than two hours on the job, I couldn't quite understand all this hullabaloo. But what I did understand was what it feels like to be passionate about what you do. And seeing a colleague that enthused about something so seemingly small, feeling empowered enough to broadcast her enthusiasm at 110 decibels in the middle of the afternoon, and receiving full approval from a supportive superior—all of that told me this might be a place to which I would really enjoy coming every weekday.

Chapter 1. Welcome to Countertransference

But before I could truly settle in and become a fully functioning member of the team, there were some important matters I needed to get straight. Most of them were in my own head.

Very early on, I was assigned a non-payment eviction case. The client's husband had temporarily lost his job, and the family had skipped paying rent for a few months. They had managed to scrape together most of the arrears, but they were still $300 or $400 short.

The normal procedure here was to make an application for a "one-shot deal," which is an emergency financial grant paid out by New York City to cover unexpected expenses, usually back rent or utilities. It's a laborious process, like all applications for public or private assistance, and I figured it would just be easier to bypass the paperwork and ask all the generous folks in the office to chip in $5 or $10 apiece, so we could resolve the problem in a couple of days. I put up a sign in the hallway requesting donations.

And the spit hit the fan.

The director called me into his office. He was irate, as was the entire office, as I learned. Once more, I didn't see what all the fuss was about. The fact that I didn't see what was wrong was the real problem.

"Look," said the boss. "What you did here was unacceptable and unprofessional. There is a way we do things in this office, in any social service office, and these procedures are in place for a reason. Once you make this job personal, make it about you and your need to set the world right, then you're no longer a case manager; you're a philanthropist. I don't ever want to see you pull a stunt like that in here again, or you're out."

"Countertransference." That was the word the director used to describe the condition under which I was operating.

Paging Sigmund Freud.

In 1910, the father of psychoanalysis was the first to define this phenomenon publicly as a therapist's emotional entanglement with a client. When Freud spoke of this "permanent problem" thereafter, it was as a caution to analysts to beware of the "countertransference lying in wait."

In letters to Carl Jung and other peers, Freud explained the dangers of a patient representing for the analyst "an object of the past onto whom past feelings and wishes are projected." Freud went so far as to warn against countertransference cases so powerful that the analyst cannot let go of the patient "and they both fall into that same dark hole of unconsciousness."

Pardon the language, but holy s—t!

15

Anyway, my boss, a clinical therapist himself, was well-versed in Freudian psychology and immune to any excuses I might have about just wanting to avoid unnecessary paperwork. The man had me sussed.

I needed to make things for this client all right in that moment, making of her one of those objects upon whom to project the sins and omissions of my own past. Or, to put it another way, to heal in the now what I couldn't heal within my own family all those decades ago: convincing my mother to stop enabling my heroin-addicted sister so she might have a chance to heal herself. Something, by the way, that my troubled sibling never managed to accomplish in her 60 years of existence.

Just some guilt I'd been lugging around for a half-century.

"Everybody who's new to this field has to learn to deal with countertransference," says a psychotherapist friend. "We all come in with baggage from our pasts. The process has to begin with knowing what's going on inside you, so you can recognize the triggers, and figure out how to check yourself when you feel them going off."

The psychotherapist says very early in her career, she found herself intimidated by, and unable to challenge, angry and strong-willed female patients.

Her supervisor pointed out the problem.

"Not every strong woman is your mother," the supervisor told her.

"Back then," she says, "I had to work especially hard on identifying the triggers that created my biases."

And, even today, after 30 years in the therapizing business, her struggle continues.

"I've got a patient who's a huge Trump fan," notes the therapist, whose values and principles lie at the other end of the political spectrum. "And when this patient goes off on the evils of Black Lives Matter and Obamacare and all the rest of it, I can feel the anxiety welling up inside me. The danger is always that it will trigger an inappropriate response.

"It's not good to not like your patients," she continues, "but I can't escape the fact that I can't stand this woman. So what I do with her is create a firm boundary. We talk about *her* experiences, what triggers *her* responses to things, and how she can approach those emotions in a different way. In the end, it has to be about the patient or the client, not us."

Here's where my wife elected to weigh in once again.

"To me, the greatest danger of countertransference," according to the most influential psychotherapist in my life, "is what happens when it isn't recognized right away. What goes on with the first client, or patient, tends to get repeated over and over again, and taints every one of your professional relationships going forward."

The good news in my case was that the message was received, and I never again did something as stupid as starting a go-fund-my-client page.

But the struggle with countertransference never ceases. Indeed, it runs like a river through just about everything I accomplished, or tried to accomplish, on the job. It was a perpetual struggle to find that safe space between maintaining professional distance and sharing a spark of humanity with people who hadn't experienced any in years. Along the way, I fought off the parallel urges to strangle my most detestable clients and befriend the most lovable.

As for those first hard days, with the requisite support from family and co-workers, particularly the savvy, veteran case manager with whom I was partnered, I found my way to the light. I can't recall ever having had an inner debate about whether or not to get out of bed and face the music.

I knew from the start that APS was the place to practice my kind of altruism.

So, for what it's worth, thank you, Rabbi.

CHAPTER 2

Orphan in the Storm

To be heroic may mean nothing more than this then, to stand in the face of the status quo, in the face of an easy collapse into the madness of an increasingly chaotic world and represent another way.

—Mike Alsford

Back in the early 1970s, I briefly dated a supple, long-haired blonde who worked in my father's office. I knew that when it came to lissome, willowy blondes, I was punching well above my weight class, and thus was not particularly surprised or upset when she announced that she was dumping me for the guy who played Mr. Moose on the *Captain Kangaroo* show.

For those born after America stopped making dishwashers, women's dresses, and most other tangible things, *Captain Kangaroo* was a hugely successful children's program in the 1950s and '60s that somehow managed to remain on network television into the mid–1980s.

The Captain, played by Bob Keeshan—who, incidentally, was the original Clarabell the Clown on *Howdy Doody*—was a genial, grandfatherly figure who played host to a variety of offbeat characters. Mr. Moose enlivened the proceedings with bad knock-knock jokes that would prompt a hail of ping-pong balls to descend from the ceiling onto the Captain's head. This kind of shtick was a laugh riot to Baby Boom toddlers like me, but not the kind that would impress willowy blondes at parties.

Nevertheless, the actor manipulating the puppet was better looking and made more money than me, so I couldn't really fault the girl for changing partners. What did hurt, however, was when she advised me that it wasn't only the actor who had stolen her heart away.

"It was the moose," she said, quite matter-of-factly. "He's cuter than you, too."

Ouch.

I relate this relatively insignificant vignette from the Third Circle of

Chapter 2. Orphan in the Storm

Dating Hell to illustrate how Adult Protective Services and I were meant for each other. Like APS, I've been known to operate from somewhere south of the 8-ball.

If human services—food stamps, Medicaid, child welfare, etc.— are the poor stepchildren of our vast governmental bureaucracy, then APS is the forgotten orphan with the lazy eye left to fend for himself in the backyard sandbox, wearing a torn t-shirt and a single shoelace-less sneaker and eating sand out of his lunch pail.

Kathleen Quinn, the frustrated yet eternally optimistic past president of the National APS Association (NAPSA) in Washington, D.C., makes no bones about the lowly public profile of APS, especially as it's reflected in the priorities of our nation's leaders.

"APS is a perpetual victim of bad timing," she says. "We can't seem to gain any traction with [those who allocate funding].... Whenever I go to testify before Congress, I have to go to considerable lengths to hide the exasperation and disappointment."

Who bears the blame for the failure at every level of our government—and, by extension, the people who elected that government—to recognize the need to assist adults in deep trouble and lacking the physical and mental ability to care for themselves?

Well, I suppose, if you were inclined to step all the way back into the dawning of a new nation, you could pin much of the blame on Daniel Boone, the late 18th century woodsman who forged the Wilderness Road through the Cumberland Gap, paving the way for westward expansion.

In so doing, Boone became the iconic representation of the "natural man," who abhorred civilization and sought only the elbow room to make his own way in the world. Unencumbered by others, requiring nothing but a gun and an axe in his two hands and the proverbial coonskin cap on his head, Daniel Boone was everyone's idealized vision of the quintessential American male.

A fanciful, if not fantastical 1784 biography, *The Adventures of Colonel Daniel Boone*, spread this hyperbolic legend throughout the land and abroad.

According to Robert Morgan, a creative writing professor at Cornell University and author of the less-hagiographic 2008 *Boone: A Biography*, Daniel himself was not at all pleased with becoming a legend in his own time. Indeed, he was disgusted with all the ways that the popular mythology had distorted the essential truths of his life.

"He probably won't shoot you"

"Nothing embitters me more in my old age," he unequivocally stated, than being thought of as the kind of man who would turn his back on his fellow man.

"Daniel Boone considered himself a common man, a family man, and helping other people was something he deeply believed in," argues Morgan. Toward the end of his life, as a means of at least partially atoning for his role in destroying the Indian wilderness habitat, Boone reputedly adopted a dozen Native American orphans.

Nevertheless, he was also keenly aware of how desperately America's intrepid pioneers needed his mythological self—which was, quite frankly, a lot more than they needed his actual self. Thus, Boone was extremely hesitant throughout his life to debunk his own myth in print.

"Settlers were about to embark on the perilous journey east to west," explains Professor Morgan, "and it was crucial to their very survival that they be able to see themselves reflected in Daniel Boone's heroic light ... as bold Indian fighters who could triumph against any adversity they would face."

Still, hundreds of years after the West was won, these discredited myths of self-reliance persist, to the point where they are now woven solidly into the fabric of our national psyche. Daniel Boone, given his relatively progressive social views, would likely be even more displeased to see how we've misinterpreted his legacy for a new century.

"In every age," concludes Robert Morgan, "people manage to twist myths for their own purposes."

Just for the myth-puncturing record, Daniel Boone stood only 5'8" in stocking feet (much shorter than Fess Parker on TV) and considered coonskin to be uncouth (he wore a beaver hat). And, oddly enough, Daniel Boone in his later years dabbled in real estate investment, and, by all accounts, was even less successful at it than Donald Trump in Atlantic City.

Further contributing to the marked failure of APS to gain a secure foothold in America is the natural tendency of people to deny unpleasant reality.

A 2018 study by Wells Fargo illustrates the depth of that denial. Some 98 percent of "older" investors, when asked if they believed that folks in their declining years could ultimately become frail and vulnerable to the point of needing outside assistance, responded in the affirmative. When the question was posed differently—Do you believe *you* could be one of those frail and vulnerable seniors?—the 98 percent response shrank all the way to 10 percent.

That's some major-league denial.

The lowly status of APS in the community, particularly pronounced among seniors, immigrants, and minorities, also stems in large part from the fear that APS, as an arm of the government, is there to take away an individual's rights, property, and dignity. These existential fears likewise run extraordinarily deep.

I have never seen it evidenced so clearly as on an episode of the cable TV show, *Hoarders*. The subject of this segment, an elderly woman living in a large house cluttered top to bottom with every conceivable form of organic and inorganic debris, was seated in a corner of the living room where there inexplicably remained a small parcel of open space. All around her were gathered family members in considerable emotional distress and professionals brought in by the cable network to alleviate the hoarding problem—a psychologist specializing in anxiety disorders, an organizational consultant, and members of a cleaning crew all trained in dealing with these horrific situations. Standing behind them was a documentary film crew—cameramen and soundmen, with their klieg lights and recording devices—all in the service of broadcasting a hoarder's degradation and shame into the nation's pristine living rooms.

Nothing about this bizarre and unsettling situation seemed to bother the woman at all. She raised hardly a peep until the psychologist mentioned that the wholesale cleanout would be done in conjunction with a referral to Adult Protective Services.

In an instant, her calm demeanor devolved into a quivering state of supreme angst. She skipped right over the anger and denial, going straight to bargaining. "Please," she implored the psychologist. "Can't you just give me two weeks [to prepare] for them?"

Patricia, a mobile outreach clinician who accompanied me on numerous home visits over the years, did not find her extreme negative reaction to be anything out of the ordinary.

"What is APS to these people?" argues Patricia. "It's strangers barging into your home with big black bags, telling you they know what's best for you. And if you don't comply, we're going to put you away somewhere. Whether this picture is true or not, the older and emotionally frailer the client, the more threatening this feels. Add in the natural fear of authority that many immigrants brought with them from the old country, the language barriers and the racial mistrust, and it all gets very dicey."

"He probably won't shoot you"

Nevertheless, a nationwide NAPSA survey conducted about 20 years ago does seem to indicate that this problem is overblown. Fewer than 10 percent of clients in that survey reported receiving APS services without their consent.

I'm not refuting those results. I will only say that the 10 percent figure does not jibe at all with my experience in New York City, where the local citizenry is not only feistier and more dyspeptic, but also more conversant with the Bill of Rights. Moreover, our nation, as a whole, over the two decades since this survey was done, has grown a lot more distrustful of government in general. I think a similar survey of APS clients in 2020 or 2021 would yield a significantly higher level of disgruntlement.

And then, there is the confusion that stems from many clients' failure to distinguish Adult Protective Services from Child Protective Services. If, in their fevered states of mind, CPS exists mainly to remove battered and neglected children from their parents, then it also stands to reason that APS exists primarily to remove them, against their wills, from the dangers in their own homes.

Such ignorance, I have to add, is not solely found among clients. When I first told friends that I was going to go to work at Adult Protective Services, many of them looked at me like I had lost my ever-lovin' mind.

"Why," wondered one of my oldest friends, "would you want to subject yourself at this point in your life to wading through all the horrible things that adults do to children?"

"No," I explained. "This is *Adult* Protective Services. We're there to help adults."

"Really.... Adult Protective Services?" my friend replied. "There is such a thing?"

Further muddying the waters is a fundamental problem that afflicts many communities across the country and extends well beyond the scope of APS: a lack of coordination and communication among all the parties tasked with aiding vulnerable adults.

"I had a case where the client was living in a massively cluttered apartment with empty cans of food all over and roaches galore," recalls Patricia. "The elderly woman was completely dehydrated, hadn't eaten in days, and couldn't get to the supermarket which was right next door to her building. The ambulance attendants who came to take her to the hospital had to have witnessed these deplorable conditions, but never documented them on their report.

"So, after holding her in the psych unit for five days, where they rehydrated and fed her, the hospital, with no idea of her home life, sent her right back into that environment with a referral to mobile outreach. Had the hospital been made aware of the whole story, they could have summoned APS [upon discharge].... As it happens, we managed to locate some family members out of the blue who didn't have a clue what was going on but very much wanted to help. Turns out the client had a ton of money [which may have contributed to the family's desire to help], so we were able to clean out the apartment without APS and get her a private-pay home health aide. But, still, this could have all gone a lot smoother if one hand were communicating with the other...."

This is the socio-political and spiritual climate in which APS has had to forge its identity. Weighed down by a couple of hundred years of mythological Boone baggage and misinformation, America's unconscionable lack of empathy for the poor and downtrodden, and a whole passel of Scarlett O'Hara–level denial, Adult Protective Services has had to negotiate a rocky path. It has been one of many fits and starts (mostly fits), and seeming triumphs that morphed into crushing disappointments. While some progress has been made in addressing the pressing needs of our most vulnerable adult citizens (i.e., all 50 states currently have at least some rudimentary form of functioning APS system), to those in the business of protecting them, progress still remains a dollar short and a day late.

Beginnings

The first discernible stirrings of a national interest in aiding at-risk adults manifested in the early-to mid–1960s, perhaps riding in on the coattails of the broader push toward a more enlightened "Great Society." Those early signals consisted mostly of scholarly treatises and studies, and the discussion and debate on the subject at that time occurred almost solely in academic circles. And it was centered virtually entirely on the protection of the elderly population.

According to NAPSA, the earliest study of APS was conducted for the National Council on Aging in 1960. This study was the basis of the first national conference held three years later. What apparently emerged from that confab was a recommendation that all organizations serving "older adults"—legal aid, medical delivery systems, social service agencies—increase their cooperative efforts.

"He probably won't shoot you"

Not exactly a ringing endorsement, and it came without any mention of the funding that would be needed to facilitate those efforts. It was a harbinger of the federal government's indifference to come.

The mid–1960s witnessed the first "demonstration projects" to gauge the effects of certain delivery systems on seniors identified as being in need of APS. By decade's end, there were fewer than 20 such community projects around the country, and their efficacy was, to put it in the kindest possible light, inconsistent.

The first real boost for APS on a national level came from the passage of Title XX of the Social Security Act of 1974. It provided permission to the states to use Social Security Block Grants (SSBG) for adults, as well as children. By the end of the '70s, about 20 states had enacted some type of legislation mandating the provision of protective services to adults.

It sounds fairly promising, but there were very large flies in the APS ointment. First, as previously noted, virtually all that money went toward the needy elderly (60-plus) population, leaving millions of 18 to-59 year olds up the creek. Second, before any of the money was spent, those ancient mythological echoes were already resonating through the halls of Congress and in academic circles.

John Regan, a prominent researcher and skeptic in the field of human services, was one of the earliest voices warning of the paternalistic nature of APS and the damage that could be inflicted on the ideal of personal autonomy by the exercise of *parens patriae* (parent of the nation) powers by the states. These powers include intervention against abusive or negligent parents and mandating legal guardians for incapacitated or disabled persons.

These misgivings have hardly diminished over the past 40 years (see Chapter 4).

Moving right along, something called the federal Prevention, Identification and Treatment of Adult Abuse Bill got passed by Congress in 1980. It was supposed to provide funding incentives to the states for the provision of APS services. The Senate followed up by making a number of recommendations along those lines.

Need I tell you that no federal action (i.e., money) was forthcoming, and those lofty expressions of Congressional concern carried all the weight of a feather in the wind?

Nevertheless, by the early 1980s, every state—in the absence of authorizing legislation—could still say with a straight face that it had established some kind of office with the responsibility to provide protective services to at least some segment of the adult population.

Throughout the 1980s, APS faced additional hurdles, aside from the longstanding paucity of federal funding. Elder abuse did become a hotter topic in research circles, but all that did for APS as a whole was push it further into irrelevance and invisibility. By 1990, those much-heralded, but modestly funded, federal block grants had likewise lost any allure they may have once possessed. Funding levels slowed to a trickle, and only 30 states were receiving *any* SSBG money to fund their APS activities.

Once the pressure began ramping up on states to increase outlays for mandated child protective services, they began cutting the already-thin slice of APS pie down to a sliver. A 1991 Congressional report noted that the average state was allocating a paltry four percent of its SSBG funding to APS. In dollar terms, according to yet another government study, states spending an average of $45.03 per client for child protection were spending just $3.80 on those over 18.

If anything, the situation got even worse from there. In the 1990s, cutbacks in supportive services such as Meals On Wheels and adult daycare robbed APS of many of the essential resources it needs to help clients remain safe and independent in their own homes.

In the two decades since, the federal government has continued to maintain radio silence and a Scrooge-like posture toward the needy adult population.

Things did appear to take a small turn for the better in the spring of 2020, as Covid ravaged the countryside. Senator Charles Grassley introduced a bill, dubbed the Emergency Support for Nursing Homes and Elder Abuse Reform Act of 2020, which contained a provision authorizing $120 million in *direct* APS funding to the states and another $60 million for Covid protection for APS workers.

Even Kathleen Quinn seemed impressed with this tentative legislative step.

"Maybe, things are starting to look up," she said.

To my mind, however, $120 million in direct aid is small potatoes. And the bill, as of this writing, is extremely short of sponsors. Even in the highly unlikely event of passage, those in the APS business know that authorization of funding and release of funding are two twains that almost never meet.

Thus, in the absence of federal guidance or funding that sees the light of day, individual states are still left mostly to their own limited devices. The current status of APS across the country could best be summed up as a hodgepodge of initiatives, with each state struggling to meet its mandate through the prism of its own social and political structures, personalities, budgetary priorities, and value systems.

Public awareness of the overall problem likewise remains low, with the possible exception of Elder Abuse, which has not lost the power to every once in a while moisten the tear ducts of a disinterested nation.

According to Joe Snyder, the former director of Philadelphia's APS system, a crucial driver was the highly-publicized case of Brooke Astor, a prominent author, socialite, philanthropist, and heiress to a vast fortune left to her by her third husband, Vincent Astor, the great-great grandson of John Jacob Astor, America's first multimillionaire.

Mrs. Astor, who passed away in 2006, according to news reports, had been diagnosed with Alzheimer's disease and suffered from multiple other ailments. Her son, Tony, appointed his mother's legal guardian, allegedly allowed her to live in squalor, without vital medications and doctors' care, while he enriched himself with income from her dwindling estate. It was all quite tawdry and ignoble, bringing to light elder abuse as a crime so far-reaching that it could devastate the lives of even our wealthiest aristocrats.

"The daily news reports of Mrs. Astor's deplorable situation were as effective as a Madison Avenue PR campaign in putting elder abuse on a par with domestic violence and child abuse in the public mind," says Snyder.

"Now, all we really needed to cement that awareness," he quips, "were some stories about the alleged abuse of Walter Cronkite."

So, this, then, is the brief, checkered history of Adult Protective Services in America. The grim task of recounting that unfortunate history, I should say, was almost as dispiriting as the history itself.

A Patchwork Crazy Quilt

According to NAPSA, there are certain aspects of APS that generally cut across geographical boundaries and are common among all 50 states.

These include some fundamental principles, guidelines and admonitions:

- Respecting the client's right of self-determination
- Employing the least restrictive alternative to ensure the client's safety
- Maintaining the family unit whenever possible
- Using community-based resources (Meals on Wheels, Medicaid home care, food stamps) rather than institutions
- Avoiding blame
- Recognizing that putting inadequate and inappropriate services in place is worse than doing nothing at all [or, as Hippocrates so succinctly put it, "First, do no harm"].

Moreover, notes former NAPSA president Quinn, in every state, APS is designated a mandated, rather than a voluntary, social service which a client can simply choose to accept or reject. Once an APS referral is taken, the crisis manager is usually required by state law to visit the home within 24 to 72 hours (depending upon the urgency of the problem) to fully investigate and determine eligibility for services. The right of self-determination notwithstanding, the client cannot dismiss APS by slamming a door in the worker's face.

In my home state, should that occur—and it does quite frequently— the worker must then go back to the home, and back again, until gaining access and obtaining enough information to file a full report.

The worker's final determination of eligibility hinges on standard case acceptance criteria, which, in New York State, number five. The absence of any of these five criterion should result in the case being summarily rejected. The first two are normally addressed at the initial intake, but the last three usually involve some digging on the part of the crisis manager during the initial visit. The criteria used in the State of New York are the following:

- That the client be 18 years of age or older;
- That the client be residing at the time of the referral in a "community setting";
- That the client have a diagnosable mental or physical impairment, which prevents him or her from having the capacity to understand and/or resolve the problem.
- That the client be "at risk in the community." Risk, as defined by APS, covers an enormous amount of ground, including, but not limited to the following: physical, sexual, financial, and emotional abuse, or neglect (including self-neglect); threatened homelessness; unhealthy or downright dangerous

living conditions (i.e., hoarding); lack of appropriate medical or psychiatric care, or inadequate health insurance; inability to manage one's "Activities of Daily Living" (i.e., toileting, feeding oneself, personal grooming, ambulation, etc.), thus necessitating some form of home or institutional care; lack of income, and lack of food. In other words, just about any problem that's really, really bad.

- And, lastly, that the client have no other source—friend, family member, social service agency—willing and able to provide the level of assistance required to resolve the situation in a favorable manner.

There are some fairly significant differences in eligibility criteria among the 50 states. New Jersey, for example, does not list the lack of credible support as an acceptance criterion. And at least one state automatically accepts every potential client over the age of 65.

According to Lori Delagrammatikas, NAPSA's affable executive director, a number of states, including Oklahoma, Oregon, and Colorado, investigate cases of abuse and/or neglect in nursing, adult, and group homes, expanding the scope of APS well beyond the "community." Massachusetts Adult Protective Services was at one time sending its workers out to assess clients in correctional facilities, which must have made for some interesting stories.

There are equally sharp variations in how states organize their APS operations. As of this writing, 36 manage APS at the state level, while 14 delegate this function to county-based organizations. Indiana, a true outlier, runs its APS function out of the District Attorney's office.

States also have widely different operating models. In New York, case managers do it all: making the initial visits, conducting interviews with the client and collateral contacts, and then putting all the services in place. Other states employ special "investigators" who perform all the upfront exploratory work and pass the cases along to case managers for implementation. Still other states have no APS case managers at all. An investigator goes out and determines whether to open or reject the case (generally within 30 to 60 days). Should the case then be accepted, it is referred to a voluntary social service or guardianship agency, provided that there is such an agency able and willing to take on the critical case. If not, Plan B calls for throwing up the hands and crying uncle.

Chapter 2. Orphan in the Storm

"It's all about funding when you get to this level," says Delagrammatikas, "and there are some states that, sadly, can't afford the expense of full-time APS case managers."

But the major differences from state to state are less about regulations, organizations, and hiring practices than the quality and quantity of the services they provide. And, here, the states are truly all over the map.

For example, some states do not provide such basic services as financial management, under which APS, as representative payee, receives the client's Social Security Disability or Supplemental Security Income checks and uses that money to pay the client's essential household bills.

More than a few states that claim to employ APS case managers haven't properly trained them. Instead, they rely on "regular caseworkers," whose primary day job is interviewing candidates for public assistance and who haven't the faintest clue as to how to proceed with a client who bathes daily in her own excrement.

"In these states," laments Kathleen Quinn, "APS is something that workers do on the side. Let's just say it's not ideal."

Additionally, many states lack the support services that we New York City APS workers have long taken for granted, such as a dedicated staff of psychiatrists from the New York State Office of Mental Health who accompany APS to client homes to conduct psychiatric evaluations. These evaluations are what provide the evidentiary basis for APS applications for personal and financial guardianships, government and private grants, representative payee-ships for Social Security checks, and many other critical benefits and entitlements. OMH psychiatrists are also pretty handy to have around when a psychotic client begins to decompensate during the home visit.

"Most APS organizations don't have regular access to psychologists or psychiatrists," says Quinn. "They might be able, on occasion, to get an on-call mental health professional to come along for support, but it's not an integral part of their [operations].... In rural areas, it's hard enough for the workers themselves to visit all the clients, let alone bringing in psychiatrists."

Training requirements, caseload levels, case longevity, and the extent of APS cooperation with local law enforcement are other aspects of the job that vary greatly state-to-state.

And, lastly, there is little, if any, uniformity regarding how individual APS organizations have handled the Covid pandemic. Some states, like New York, have been sending workers into the field. Others have had their workers sheltering in place, communicating by clients strictly by phone. Some states allowed workers to return to their offices to share their thoughts and feelings and maintain staff camaraderie; others are limiting staff contact to the virtual world.

Oddly enough, according to sources, the efficacy of some states' APS functions doesn't necessarily equate to their overall commitment to a strong social safety net.

For example, Texas, a state not known for its generosity or equity in the delivery of human services, is said to have one of the finest APS operations in the country. Another, among the bluer of the blue northeastern states, is still said to be "winging it" as it attempts to field a viable APS presence.

While all this goes on, case referrals across the country continue to flow like a mighty stream, arriving from anywhere and everywhere.

Many clients self-refer. These include clients who are fully aware that they're in deep trouble, and those who aren't in any trouble, but imagine they are. I prefer self-referential cases.

If they're genuine, at the very least you've got a client who desires your assistance. And if it isn't a legitimate problem, you can reject the case before you've officially opened it. But quite often, in the investigation of an unsubstantiated referral, real problems lurking beneath the surface and requiring immediate attention are discovered. Like the elderly woman who phones in a false complaint about a thieving home attendant but is found to have a ne'er-do-well nephew who's been robbing her blind for years. Or the client who imagines his kindly landlord is the incarnation of Satan but has neglected to have the three-pound tumor on the back of his neck biopsied.

Other referrals come from family, friends, or neighbors, named or anonymous, voluntary social services organizations, hospital social workers, visiting nurses, clinical psychologists, local legislators, and law enforcement officials. Most referrals are legit but lacking in accuracy or detail. Others are what we call "CYA" (cover your ass) referrals, which often come from other social service professionals too busy or too lazy to do their homework and quite comfortable dumping their problematic cases at the APS landfill.

Back in my day, APS case management entailed a modicum of paperwork and a lot of good, old-fashioned human interaction. All documentation has long since been computerized, and with that has come a bevy of new regulations involving the processing and sharing of data.

Chapter 2. Orphan in the Storm

Client caseloads, at least in New York, continue to rise. By all accounts, APS crisis management—even sans Covid—appears to be more daunting and less enjoyable (if I can use that word) than it was 15 years ago.

And that's unfortunate.

CHAPTER 3

Hidden Figures

Esse est percipi" (To exist means to be perceived).
—George Berkeley, 18th century philosopher

Tucked away behind a large multi-family stucco house on a leafy, quiet little street in Queens was a tool shed. From the outside, it looked like any other place in which one would store band saws, lathes, and hand drills. The white paint was peeling, and the door hinges were rusty. But on the inside, this was clearly no ordinary shed. The interior decoration featured a slightly soiled Oriental rug, a love seat, and a couple of old arts & crafts chairs. There was a small kitchen area, a butcher-block dining table, and a few prints on the walls. All of this befitting the fact that the shed was home to a gimlet-eyed, middle-aged single mother and her disabled pre-teen daughter.

Indeed, in modern-day parlance, one might have been tempted to label this a "she-shed," the female correlative of the man-cave. A place where a woman (or women) could find a separate peace and tranquility and pursue their interests in the total absence of male influence. This might well have been the case in this shed were it not for the family of raccoons who had also made themselves at home in and around the premises. While these peripatetic raccoons tended to move about a lot and mostly minded their own business when they were nesting alongside the shed, their co-tenancy made it extraordinarily difficult for a mother and daughter to maintain any sense of feminine tranquility.

Making the overall situation even less tranquil, the owners of the main house, who had given the client and daughter a roof over their heads, were in the process of selling the property. Thus, all the occupants of the shed, human and otherwise, were faced with incipient eviction.

This was the first home visit I remember making as an Adult Protective Services case manager. As was the custom back then, I was in the company of my supervisor and a fellow case manager, who were there to show me the ropes. The client, who clearly preferred a shed with raccoon roommates to the horrors of the New York City family shelter system, had a righteous beef with APS. Her previously-assigned case manager—the man who had my job before me—was considerably less than diligent about working his cases. This client had not seen her APS worker in months, and she was justifiably miffed. She made no effort to curb her acerbic tongue.

"Frankly, I don't give a f—k who you are," she greeted me. "As long as you're not the last guy."

In an eviction case like this—a "defenseless holdover" in which the tenant has no practicable legal defense—there generally isn't much APS can do, aside from helping him or her find decent, affordable shelter somewhere else (there really isn't any such readily-available housing) or attempting to buy the client a few weeks or months in housing court in which to figure out the next move.

This client was not one to wait around for the legal process to play out. Following my initial visit, she and her daughter took off for parts unknown. Hopefully, they managed to make their way to family or friends who could house them in a safer environment. In any case, I never saw either of them again.

What is so unremarkably remarkable about such APS cases is how they tend to hide in plain sight, or just slightly out of sight, in the middle of a teeming metropolis like New York City. I don't believe any residents on that block had the faintest notion that they had neighbors living in a raccoon-infested tool shed only steps away from their wraparound porches.

An even more glaring example of this phenomena could be found in the tony precincts of Manhattan's Upper West Side, where my client, a retired handyman at a luxury condo building on Central Park West, lived in a large studio apartment deeded to him by management. Here this common man resided among society's super-elites—rock stars, corporate chieftains, European princes, and trust fund babies—who apparently lacked the slightest clue that their handyman neighbor was a prolific hoarder of automobile parts. Carburetors, fan belts, and transmissions were stacked up in his studio, floor to ceiling, like Saltines in an unopened box. The client had somehow managed to carve out a narrow path from door to fire escape window, but the remainder of the available space was given over to Detroit's detritus. Were this a battle between man and machine, the machines had long ago declared victory.

Because the client was not hoarding any organic material that would emit a discernible odor and was very careful to make sure no one was standing around when he opened his door, building management had yet to discover what was going on amidst all the gilded splendor. Thus, the client was not facing a risk of eviction and there was no immediate basis for APS action. The client told me his plan was to move all this machinery into a garage at a private home he owned upstate.

"If you think this apartment is full of stuff," he said with a big grin, "you should see what I've got going on up there."

I shuddered just a little in envisioning what could be more cluttered than this but took some pleasure in imagining the reaction of his hoity-toity neighbors as they watched 30 tons of corroded auto parts being carried out of their Art Deco dwelling in the middle of the afternoon. Not to mention the impact of such a sight on those fashionable Upper West Side property values.

Another group of clients who tended to remain deep in shadow and out of sight were the undocumented aliens, the "illegals," who had sound reasons, apart from mental illness, for staying well out of the public eye. The price they would pay for visibility was their homes, their families, and sometimes their very lives.

In New York, known for the generosity of its social safety net, the undocumented had very little access to that net; the totality of their entitlement consisting of emergency Medicaid, a limited form of health insurance that pays for the treatment of one ailment, say, a broken leg, but will cover no further medical costs. And, of course, the undocumented had access to Adult Protective Services when everything else had spiraled out of control. Otherwise, these folks—good folks, mostly—were on their own in attempting to survive in a society that largely reviles them.

I remember Arshad, a single, middle-aged Pakistani, who, like nearly all my undocumented clients, lived alone, below ground, in a ratty basement studio. It was furnished with articles reclaimed from the street: a sooty old rug, a sofa that was mostly springs augmented by a few thin strands of fabric, and a TV broadcasting the latest news from Karachi through blurred, squiggly lines. Arshad emerged from that basement only to work as an itinerant house painter and for daily prayer at his local mosque. He paid his rent and his other bills on time, and, as far as I could determine, was doing nobody any harm.

I got called in by a city hospital in Queens, as the client was non-compliant with his out-patient treatment and medications to manage his schizophrenia. It was my task to convince him to come out of hiding for something other than work and prayer.

The client was a taciturn fellow whose trust in government authority was about what you'd expect from an undocumented Muslim in post–9/11 New York with a severe and persistent mental illness. Yet, he agreed to allow me to escort him to his monthly appointments at the hospital's mental health clinic, where he received his shots and some talk therapy.

On the subway to and from the hospital, the client and I looked quite the Mutt-and-Jeff pair—the 5'8" Jewish crisis manager and the 6'3" bearded Muslim schizophrenic. Finding some common ground for normal conversation was difficult, to say the least, but the two of us muddled through, and eventually developed a rapport, based on a mutual disdain for subway-dwelling Norwegian sewer rats and a joint claim to Abraham as spiritual father.

I closed Arshad's case once he was back in regular treatment. I sincerely hope he stuck with it and stayed out of trouble, as the thought of this client facing deportation in a floridly psychotic state was not a pleasant one.

I would venture that the majority of my clients during my APS tenure were similarly invisible within their own communities. It almost seemed like the level of gloom and despair enveloping these clients was inversely proportional to the concern of those around them. The more deplorable the conditions, it appeared, the more oblivious the neighbors. This caused me at times to wonder just who were the more dysfunctional—the clients or their fellow New Yorkers to whom they didn't exist.

Then again, I thought of myself and the neighbors in my apartment building in Queens. I have not been in every one of their homes. The engineer on the second floor, a seemingly conventional fellow, could be hoarding auto parts or something more objectionable, for all I knew. Better, perhaps, not to judge thy neighbors too harshly.

Clinical psychologists and most mental health professionals do not find the community's behavior in these situations to be at all unusual, or particularly egregious.

Dr. Frank McAndrew, a psychology professor at Knox College in Illinois who has studied the impact of social isolation on astronauts, Antarctic explorers, and others living in extreme solitude, says mounds of data support the finding that people in large cities are far less likely to be involved with others in their communities, especially those others who are in the most desperate need of concrete and/or emotional support.

"It's largely out of necessity," McAndrew says. "People living on top of each other are overwhelmed with navigating their way through their own lives. It's very hard for them to be monitoring what goes on outside their circle. Plus, basic norms of privacy are [stricter] in cities than in small towns and villages."

On the plus side, however, an urban community is less likely than its rural counterpart to ostracize those secluded souls living in pain and squalor.

"Being ignored, having your neighbors be indifferent to your existence," concludes McAndrew, "is certainly preferable to having them banish you from their society."

While all this may be a hard reality of urban American life, it does not address the underlying moral conundrum. I came away from my years at APS in the confirmed belief that us city folk could do a better job of looking out for one another and blowing the whistle when something does not look right.

Nevertheless, this becomes particularly difficult with at least one large and rapidly growing demographic that has turned hiding in the shadows into an art form.

Jane Bardavid, a Manhattan psychotherapist who ran a mental health clinic for seniors for many years, says this group of needy adults tends to fall into two general categories.

"We saw a lot of elderly parents in their 80s or early 90s who had taken on the tremendous responsibility of caring for their severely disabled 50- or 60-year old children," she says. "What happens here is mom and dad bond together to fulfill an all-consuming job that, by its very nature, creates total social isolation. And, then, when one of the parents dies, the full-time caregiver role becomes just too overwhelming and the surviving parent ends up turning to us."

The worst of these cases ultimately get turned over to APS.

The other category—victims of elder abuse—represents a more serious societal problem and a bigger challenge for the social service community.

"Here, the social isolation is not driven by necessity, but by shame," says Bardavid. "We saw some of that at the clinic, mostly emotional and financial abuse by their children. But it's the deep shame that keeps these victims from ever coming forward to seek help."

If and when social services or law enforcement comes riding to the rescue, the victim invariably denies the problem up and down the line.

The myriad forms of elder abuse that I encountered on the job could be pretty well summed up in Monty Python's comic masterpiece in which a third party is aghast at the awful treatment undergone by an abuse survivor.

"But you say he nailed your head to the floor," says the third party. To which the victim replies, "Yes, but he didn't know me."

And, finally, there are those hidden seniors who fall into categories all their own.

Case in point is a referral that a former colleague, Joellen, received back in the early 2000s. Here a concerned neighbor, catching a whiff of something afoot, was willing to report her suspicions to Adult Protective Services. Unfortunately, she succeeded only in opening a Pandora's box of dysfunction that might have been better left shut.

The referral source expressed worries about a bunch of wires strung out in front of the client's house. Said client, a Caucasian male in his late 80s, did not fit the usual profile. He was regularly seen jogging up and down the block in the morning and appeared to be in fine fettle. He had a son who lived with him on and off, but, again, nothing about their relationship presented as out of the ordinary.

When the younger man let Joellen into the home, the situation became a little clearer. There were more wires strung about the foyer and living room area.

"May I ask what all these wires are for?" she inquired.

"Absolutely," replied the son. "They're for communicating with all the planets I'm in touch with."

Meanwhile, the client sat quietly in his favorite living room chair, seemingly not bothered at all by his son's interplanetary fantasy.

"The old man appeared to be totally okay," recalls Joellen. "He was appropriately groomed and dressed and did not present as malnourished or dehydrated. I took a look around, and the rest of the house was in pretty good shape. So far, all I had was a delusional son, and he didn't seem to be a danger to himself or his father."

The son also made it a point to note his mother's ashes in an urn on the fireplace mantle. He indicated that he and his father felt her presence in the home every day.

"She was the light of our lives," he said. "But you should look in the freezer," he added. "She is with us there, too."

"He probably won't shoot you"

Joellen walked into the kitchen and ever-so-slowly opened the freezer door. And, just as the son had cautioned, there was Mom, in the form of a large human head wrapped in tin foil. It had its own shelf, and it jarred this experienced social worker to her professional and personal core.

"I really tried to remain calm," says Joellen, "but this was way out of my experience."

This was not a case like, say, that of Ted Williams's children, who cryogenically preserved their father's head for future transplant to a major league-ready body. This was simply a father and son who did not want to part with a major part of their loved one.

Joellen somehow managed to hold it together until she got back to the office and collapsed into the arms of a trusted colleague. After a good cry, they discussed strategy. First off, the client himself had demonstrated no evidence of being mentally or physically disabled or neglected in any way. The client presented as particularly nimble in sidestepping the wires on the floor and was at no significant risk in his home.

To be sure, the head in the freezer was a cause for concern, but, if anything, this was an issue for the Health Department or, perhaps more appropriately, for law enforcement authorities. In the State of New York, it is not legal to decapitate a corpse prior to cremation, and no legitimate crematorium will accept a headless body. Thus, in this highly unusual case, it would appear that the family went ahead and took these sensitive matters into its own hands. This would further suggest the type of unsavory, late-night goings-on in the fireplace or the backyard barbeque pit that one would not encounter outside of an old Vincent Price horror movie.

Enough said.

And, finally, the son's belief that he was in contact with extraterrestrials, strange as that seemed, presented as no more than a harmless affectation.

So once again, there was no strict procedural basis for opening an APS case, and thus the neighbors remained blissfully ignorant of what lurked within a freezer compartment.

Joellen, still creeped out nearly 20 years later by this real-life Addams Family tableau, doubts she will ever be able to get the image of that frozen head completely out of her own head.

"How I came into work the next day and went out on another home visit, I will never know," she says. "All I can say is that at APS, you have to be ready for whatever awaits you on the other side of the door."

She was referring to the front door, but such guidance would certainly apply to a freezer, a closet, and every other door in a client's home.

My response here was a full-throated *Amen*.

CHAPTER 4

Damned If You Do....

*Until you've lost the ability to make rational decisions,
you retain the right to make dumb ones!*
—From the New Jersey Department
of Human Services website, as regards the role of APS

*How strange that the nature of life is change, yet the
nature of human beings is to resist change.*
—Elizabeth Lesser

The Rev. Al Sharpton, a highly polarizing figure in a highly polarized nation, has at various times in his long and disputatious career been a lot of things to a lot of people: a vocal and tireless advocate for the civil rights of millions of African Americans; a cynical race hustler (as exemplified in the unsavory Tawana Brawley affair in the 1980s); an FBI informant; a Baptist minister; a failed presidential candidate; and, most recently, esteemed host of his own nightly talk show on the MSNBC cable TV network.

Oh, and add one more role: Adult Protective Services gadfly.

In taking on APS, the "Rev" (as he's widely known) was not without company. Sharpton's National Action Network was but one of a number of civil rights advocacy groups around the country to have targeted APS as a source of oppressive governmental intrusion into the lives of already marginalized Black citizens.

I never envisioned my organization in this unflattering light, but there is no mistaking the fact that APS sometimes treads an elusive and slippery path between people's rights of self-determination and giving them a helping hand. And when it comes to minority communities, this dichotomy can be even more problematic.

Joe Snyder, the former director of Philadelphia's APS unit, acknowledges that pushback from the civil rights community has been yet another factor weighing against widespread public acceptance of

40

APS's legitimate role in making communities safer, especially urban communities.

"Philadelphia is a major city of color, and, yes, you would constantly hear criticism [of racial bias] coming from activist groups. Some minority clients, particularly those in the 18 to 59 [age] population, viewed us that way. They even feared us, at least to some extent. Those of us on the ground just did our jobs, but the perception, I think, is still very much out there."

Nevertheless, the Right Reverend Al, in his civil rights agitator persona, has been known to see oppression in all the wrong places. A prime example of this is a case on which I consulted 15 years ago.

The client was an elderly black woman living in an uptown Manhattan housing project where she cared for her toddler granddaughter. Their apartment was in deplorable condition, bathed in filth and infested with bedbugs, and the New York City Housing Authority, having been made aware of the condition of the home, had initiated eviction proceedings. When I and a colleague made an initial visit, the client was not unhappy to see us and graciously led us into her living room. The child, for her part, was well-behaved and thoroughly adorable. They were seemingly the kind of clients who would make for a stress-free afternoon: easy-going people with an easily solvable problem.

But, sadly, there was another cause for concern that we couldn't, in all good conscience, ignore. Those would be the maggots gnawing on grandma's left leg.

The leg itself was apparently dead, as the client was feeling no pain, but my partner and I nevertheless urged her in the strongest terms to seek immediate medical attention. Note that we did not call 911 or otherwise attempt to coerce the client into seeking such care. However, given what we had witnessed, we would have been seriously remiss in keeping quiet.

A close relative of the client, who did not live in the home, was advised of APS's involvement in the case and did not take kindly to it. While we saw our role here as encouraging healthy behavior and keeping grandmother and granddaughter from losing their apartment, this family member was said to have viewed our presence in the household as a civil rights violation on the part of some governmental busybodies. He managed to attract the Rev. Sharpton's attention and enlist him in his anti–APS crusade.

This particular family member's personal motives will never be fully known, although sometime after a heavy-duty cleaning was accomplished and the APS case closed, he did get back to someone in the organization about the possibility of suing the agency on the "Judge Judy" show so that everyone could walk away from this little episode with some cash.

Sharpton's motives, I suspect, were mixed. He has always been fond of publicity, good or bad, but more likely for him, this case echoed the tragic, and totally avoidable, death of Eleanor Bumpurs.

Like the client described above, Ms. Bumpurs was an elderly, disabled African American living in a New York City housing project and facing eviction. She was reported to the police as an "EDP"—an emotionally disturbed person—threatening to throw boiling lye or use a knife on anyone attempting to carry out the eviction order.

When the confused and terrified woman refused to open her home to the cops, they burst through the door and shot the poor lady twice with a 12-gauge single-barreled shotgun. The cop who fired the gun was charged with manslaughter and acquitted.

"What happened to Eleanor Bumpurs was still very much on the minds of civil rights workers at the time, but their concern, at least as regards this situation, was clearly misplaced," says an APS supervisor closely connected to this case. She says Sharpton went so far as to take up the matter with Mayor Michael Bloomberg's office and with other high-ranking city officials.

"But what struck me as really bizarre was when the Rev, himself, called me on the phone, threatening me and accusing APS of bringing in the bedbugs."

Neither the Reverend Sharpton, nor anyone on his staff at NAN, responded to multiple requests for comment on this 15-year-old story.

I can't say I blame them.

But race is only one flashpoint in the ongoing debate over the civil and privacy rights of adult clients.

Lori Delagrammatikas of NAPSA says APS units across the country have also been getting serious flak from victims of domestic violence and people with disabilities. The issue here is "mandated reporting," or the legal responsibility of social service agencies and educators to report cases of suspected abuse to law enforcement.

Mandated reporting has long been a universal requirement for all agencies providing services to children. It also applies to nearly every state APS organization, with the odd exception of New York, which to the dismay of some, has declined to designate its county APS units as mandated reporters of physical and sexual abuse of adults.

Chapter 4. Damned If You Do....

"It's an issue that is increasingly a subject of discussion and debate in APS circles," says Delagrammatikas. "Many domestic violence survivors and disabled people consider it audacious on the part of government to make these intimate details of their private lives public."

But where the rubber truly meets the road with regard to the rights of APS clients is the OGA, short for an "Order to Gain Access."

According to a March 1987 Administrative Directive to all New York State Social Services Commissioners, APS is authorized to petition a court for permission to enter a client's home without the consent of the occupants.

Kind of like a search warrant.

This extreme step requires reasonable cause for APS to believe that the client is in need of its services, and that all non-legal efforts to gain access—through family, friends, neighbors, clergymen, etc.—have been exhausted. The person denying access could be a self-neglecting client or a caregiver suspected of abusing or exploiting the client.

Those participating in this legally sanctioned form of breaking-and-entering include the APS crisis manager, the locksmith who removes the door lock and replaces it upon completion of the process, an Office of Mental Health staff psychiatrist, and a couple of NYPD officers to provide security.

There is a certain solemnity that often attends this exercise in governmental intervention: a feeling among the participants that, perfectly legal though it is, an OGA is something antithetical to the ideals of a democratic society. I don't want to go all Patrick Henry over this, but after an OGA, a cleansing shower is highly recommended.

In my seven long years on the job, I petitioned for only two OGAs and felt compelled to execute just one. But that was quite enough.

The client was a single woman of about 45 with a reported diagnosis of schizophrenia, living with her aged immigrant father and primary caregiver. It was he who denied APS access on several occasions, despite my warnings that if he continued to refuse, APS might be forced to take matters into its own hands. He neither responded to a worker at the door nor repeated phone calls. He had no relationship with any of his neighbors, and I could not locate anyone in the area who might have some influence over his behavior.

The client's brother, a prominent Florida attorney, advised me that, as a child growing up in the home, he, himself, had been physically and emotionally abused by his father. And it was the brother's strong belief that the old man was treating his disabled sister in a similar fashion.

43

"He probably won't shoot you"

For me, the brother's fears, coupled with the hostility of the father and his refusal to allow his daughter to be seen by APS, were sufficient to take this case to a judge.

On the morning of the OGA, we all showed up at the apartment. After a few minutes of beseeching the old man to take this last opportunity to do the right thing, he finally opened the door and let all of us inside.

It was yet another shining example of NBR—never believe the referral.

I don't recall the reasons the man gave for blocking access, but once we were already in there, he was polite, courteous, and almost friendly. We spoke in his bedroom, which, like the rest of the home, was impeccably clean and well-furnished. The man, who was in his mid–80s and hailed from somewhere in Eastern Europe, denied ever abusing his daughter or his estranged son, adding that he didn't know what would prompt him to make unfounded and outrageous allegations. My takeaway here was that the truth, in all likelihood, lay somewhere between the conflicting stories of a father and son.

More important, the client, who spoke privately with the psychiatrist in the living room, denied any problem whatsoever. She claimed her father was a good man who had never physically or sexually abused her, and there were no obvious bruises, welts or other marks on her body that would indicate otherwise. She said she had long been under appropriate psychiatric care, providing her psychiatrist's name and contact information, and showing the OMH doctor all her bottled medications, with which she reported being fully compliant.

All that stress and solemnity, for nothing.

The next day, I phoned the brother, who said he was relieved to have been mistaken about what was going on in the home.

"Maybe my father has changed," he concluded.

The other OGA application, which a judge approved, was filed on behalf of a client who had advised me on the phone that he had never allowed another human being to enter his threshold, and had no intention of having that tradition desecrated by the likes of APS.

The referral referenced a potential hoarding hazard and the client's strange behavior toward his neighbors.

Anyway, on the day before the execution of the order, the client called to offer a compromise: in lieu of allowing a home visit, he would be willing to come into our office and submit to a psychiatric evaluation to prove he had the capacity to make his own decisions.

Chapter 4. Damned If You Do....

It seemed like a fair solution. The client showed up at the appointed time and sat for the evaluation. He was all sweaty and restless, as super-solitary middle-aged men tend to be when in the presence of others. But he also presented as intelligent, articulate, and reasonably sound of mind. He knew the president's name, how to count from 100 backwards by seven, and how to draw a clock that displays 2 p.m. He was just another American hermit; no need here for extraordinary measures.

And I closed his case.

I was far from the only APS employee with a moral aversion to OGAs. A former supervisor in Manhattan with libertarian tendencies and a compassionate soul had a knack for avoiding them.

One elderly client, accused of spreading her poop on the doors of neighbors she didn't like, was repeatedly refusing access to her assigned APS worker. An OGA seemed imminent. This supervisor elected to take one last stab at preventing it.

"I arrive at her apartment and, as I expected, she yells at me through the locked door to get the hell away," relates the supervisor.

"So I say to her through the door, 'Please let me explain why I'm here.... I heard about how the neighbors called the police on you, and how they took you away to the psychiatric ward and held you there. I'm so sorry that happened to you. I'm here to make sure that nothing that terrible happens to you again.'"

The upshot: the client let the supervisor in to conduct an assessment, after which she confined her bathroom behaviors strictly to the bathroom, thus making the carrying out of the OGA unnecessary.

Perhaps there is no more important skill on a case manager's tool belt than making a client believe that the two of them are playing on the same team.

"These are people looking, above all, to have their feelings, no matter how crazy they are, validated," explains a therapist with long experience assisting APS. "They need to believe in this vision they have of themselves as not being pathetic. I'm not suggesting that their case managers buy into that vision or sell them a bill of goods, but if you're going to break through that initial wall of resistance, the client has to see the worker as an ally and not an adversary."

I had a few cases of my own that required a gentle, soft-sell approach to keep the matter out of court.

There was a grandmother in her early 70s, a voracious hoarder in midtown Manhattan, who was refusing entry to a stranger. There was only one man to whom she would allow access to her cluttered fortress, but, fortunately, that was the building maintenance man. He reported to me that the apartment was, indeed, piled high with enough *shmatas* to stock Filene's Basement, but did not represent a fire hazard or a public health emergency.

Later, I interviewed the client at a neighborhood delicatessen. She was a retired certified public accountant with a small army of grand-children up in New England and a charming demeanor. Over corned beef and pastrami, she convinced me, nearly beyond a reasonable doubt, that she had the necessary marbles to handle her own affairs. She did acknowledge being a "pack rat," which suggested a lack of insight into her own deep-seated problem. But she was clearly not some dod-dering old lady who needed to have her apartment invaded by social workers.

So much for that OGA.

But not all APS staffers viewed OGAs as an inherent infringement on individual liberty. Some saw a quick solution to an otherwise impos-sible problem.

"As long as the reasons were valid and the workers had tried other options, I never hesitated signing off on an OGA," says a former supervi-sor. "To me, it was a lot less restrictive alternative than, say, a guardian-ship application, which can take a year. An OGA was no big deal. We did quite a few of them."

While I would disagree that conducting an OGA is no big deal, it is sometimes a necessity to ensure the client's health and safety.

Like, for example, this old hoarding case.

"The client's apartment was up on the fourth floor, but I smelled it all the way down to the foyer on the ground floor," says Sylvia, a former colleague in Queens. "The neighbors [and the New York City Housing Authority] were in an uproar. I tried getting in three times, to no avail. I didn't feel I had any choice but an OGA....

"When we got there, the two cops managed to open the door about three inches, and behind it you could glimpse the enormous amount of garbage piled up inside. Through the crack in the doorway, I could also see the client, an elderly woman with long, blonde hair. She hadn't been trying to keep us out of the place. She was just too feeble to get to the door and pry it open....

"Anyway, the psychiatrist, talking to her on the other side of the door, got her to agree to go to the hospital. But the client was shaped a lot like the Pillsbury Doughboy, and we couldn't squeeze her body through that small opening. After a lot of effort, the cops finally got the door opened another few inches, and were able to get hold of the woman and slide her out by the shoulders."

The client left Sylvia with her house keys and a plea to take care of her seven cats, who resided somewhere amidst all the flotsam and jetsam. Two kindly employees from Animal Control, after a long search, were able to dig out the mangy cats, miraculously still alive in the wreckage. The HDC took place without the client, who remained in the psych ward while the crew carried out approximately 12 tons of accumulated waste material.

I counted nearly 500 bags of refuse out on the street because I was the worker at the scene on days one and two of the cleaning, covering for Sylvia, who was on a much-needed vacation.

The client eventually returned to her apartment, the invasion of privacy having been a small price to pay for a brand-new, garbage-free lifestyle and seven healthy and happy pussycats.

...And Damned If You Don't

For a charm of powerful trouble/Like a hell broth, boil
and bubble.
—William Shakespeare, "Macbeth"

Among healthcare and social service workers on the North Shore of Long Island, the three elderly sisters had achieved some notoriety as "The Three Witches."

As in the three witches who prophesized the rise and fall of Macbeth in Shakespeare's immortal tale of unspeakable crime and the punishment which ineluctably follows.

Those three hags, in their "filthy trappings," show up frequently across the generations, in many guises and cultures—as mythological Fates, voodoo priestesses, vengeful hippies, murderous Goth schoolgirls....

And rejected APS clients.

Tom, a physical therapist contracted by a local hospital's home care unit, showed up at their home to do an evaluation of one of the sisters, who had just been discharged after treatment for a major stroke. He was not aware that three people inhabited the dwelling, which, from the outside, appeared to him to be a typically well-kept piece of suburban frontier America.

"When I got through the front door," recounts Tom, "the patient insisted I take her medical history in the foyer, where she'd set up two folding chairs a few feet apart. I told her it was crucial that I see the rest of the house. She was very resistant at first, but I kept plugging away, and reluctantly she brought me into the living room, which was cluttered with dirty clothes, boxes and bags. The woman walked with a quad cane and it must have been difficult for her to get into her hospital bed, which was surrounded by a debris field on the floor.

"At the kitchen door, there was another elderly woman standing there—this was the second sister. She was sloshing around in plastic

48

bags wrapped to her ankles which were capturing all the fluid that was leaking from her edema. The third sister was lingering in the back of the kitchen. All three looked to be in poor shape.

"But bad as it seemed, it got much worse when I entered the kitchen," Tom continues. "That part of the house was the most disgusting ... dirty dishes piled up on the counter and in the sink, boxes and boxes of open food, cockroaches everywhere. I asked to see the bathroom, which was in the basement. Turns out the bathroom was the only clean room in the home, but it was all for naught, because none of the sisters could get down the stairs to use it."

Tom phoned up his supervisor, and reported his findings. He learned that the three sisters had been frequent flyers in the system, with Medicare bath aides, nurses, and medical technicians coming and going for years. But what really shocked the pants off this experienced and compassionate PT was being told that Adult Protective Services had also been in the home on multiple occasions, and had done nothing to relieve the deplorable conditions in which the family lived.

"I was informed that APS had determined that the sisters posed no dangers to themselves, so they had closed the case," concludes Tom. "For the life of me, I couldn't understand how they could walk away from this scene. I'm well-versed in the concept of self-determination, and I'm guessing that all three sisters had [passed psychiatric] evaluations. But, there just had to be some way for APS to get involved here. Three sisters in their late 70's and 80's with severe physical disabilities and living in squalor. I mean, really ... what does it take to get some action?"

I empathize with Tom's frustration, and with a grisly case like that of the Three Witches, I'd have been inclined to take a more aggressive tack, a work-around to bypass any sticky civil rights concerns and get the job done. But having been on the other side of the fence, I'm reluctant to judge other APS workers for exercising more caution.

Sometimes there's just no getting around that pesky Fourth Amendment.

There are any number of other nuanced situations which end, inevitably, with even the most dedicated APS workers having no option other than to shrug it off and move on to the next case.

Such was a situation that arose in Queens in the winter of 2019, which featured a woman living in a big old house left to her by her parents. The boiler was busted, and the house was cold enough to refrigerate a vat of cottage cheese.

A social worker from a large non-profit agency who received the initial referral passed it off to APS, figuring they would assist the woman in finding safe, temporary housing, while they worked out a way to raise the temperature of her present residence above 40 degrees Fahrenheit. The problem was that the deed to the house had not yet been put in the client's name, and thus APS was not at liberty to facilitate repairs or perform any structural work within the home.

They rejected the case without ever having entered the premises.

The baffled social worker reached out to several other agencies, and was told essentially the same thing: if the house doesn't legally belong to the client, there is nothing that can be done.

"This seemed to me to be completely insane," she says. "You've got a woman half-frozen to death in her home, and, understandably, not wanting to go to a homeless shelter, and nobody can do a thing to help her.... At the very least, I'd have thought APS might find the poor woman an interim place to hole up for the winter. But there are rules and regulations that govern these things and even APS is not [immune] to them."

The social worker was henceforth instructed by her own superior to drop the case, to which she initially objected.

"I remember we had a big argument over it," she says. "But, ultimately, I had no choice but to back off.... I have no idea what happened to this client."

Other cases just leave an APS crisis manager shaking his or her head, like a middle-aged client of mine in Brooklyn. She was a single woman who had been drinking herself into a daily stupor for 20 years. At age 53 or 54, she possessed the careworn mien of a woman of 80.

I recall she lived in a large house with her older brother, a gentle man who had done everything within his limited power to get his little sister to pull herself together. He remembered Eleanor as she used to be—a professor of sociology, a devoted daughter, a loving sister, someone with a future. APS was his final resort.

On my initial home visit in the late afternoon, I caught the client in her full state of inebriation: a fall-down drunk, crying and slobbering incoherently.

I returned a few days later in the morning, between a hearty breakfast and a liquid lunch. Sober, Eleanor was highly articulate, self-reflective, and a surprisingly engaging conversationalist. We talked about Trobriand Islanders, our dear-old college days, and what that first daily shot of Johnny Walker Black feels like going down.

I brought a psychiatrist along on the next visit to conduct an evaluation. The client was only one or two sheets to the wind, clear enough to state her intention to continue drinking to excess, like Nicolas Cage in *Leaving Las Vegas.*

The psychiatrist provided a recommendation for an Article 81 personal guardian, although I hadn't requested a guardianship.

"What is a guardian going to do for this client?" I inquired of the psychiatrist. "Put her in rehab? Even if that were possible, even if by some miracle she would consent, she's been through rehab so many times in the past 20 years that they don't even bother checking her in anymore."

The shrink agreed.

"Truth is, I didn't know what else to write down," she confessed with a sigh.

I told the brother that I was closing his sister's case and watched the lights go out in his eyes.

"I guess that's about all anyone can do for Eleanor," he said. "Thanks for your interest."

Another such case involved a troubled family in Queens: the middle-aged father, who was the client, his wife, his mother, and his 20-something son, who suffered from bipolar disorder, diagnosed but untreated. When I arrived, the three elders were in the kitchen. The son was asleep in the next room. Everyone was tip-toeing about on tenterhooks.

"Please keep your voice way down," whispered the client. "I don't want to wake Donald."

The client was unquestionably compos mentis, in full control of his mind and capable of making his own decisions.

I could argue persuasively that the decisions he had been making to date regarding what to do about Donald were really bad ones. But, again, the law allows every adult the freedom to make horrendous choices.

As it was, the lives of the three other people in the home revolved entirely around Donald's disposition at any given moment. Any deviation from the status quo, according to the client, might cause Donald to flip his lid.

The house itself was in disarray, inside and out. There were major electrical and plumbing issues, falling plaster from the ceiling and gaping holes in the walls. The kitchen table, upon which rested a small mountain of garbage, was the first thing you noticed upon entering the home. These were the conditions that prompted the APS referral from an anonymous neighbor.

"We could assist you in having your home cleaned out and maybe making some small repairs," I advised the client, in my softest, quasi-therapeutic voice. "I think it would make things a lot more bearable for all of you."

"That would be impossible," the man said. "My son would never allow it."

While Donald may have had the disease, it was his family who bore the brunt of it. Together, they had chosen a path of peaceful co-existence under one roof, and the price they paid for that highly tenuous peace was their freedom.

The client, whose face registered a mixture of deflation and fear, in equal measure, understood the ramifications of his inaction much better than I.

"I would like for you to leave us alone right now," he said.

With an obdurate client who registered no signs of a disability, I acceded to the request, rejected the case, and wished this poor sad sack all the best.

On some future day, I reckoned, someone else would be standing in the kitchen in the wake of the ceiling having come crashing down on the family and wondering how and why APS had been so derelict in its duty.

All the above-cited cases are, to varying degrees, nuanced and shaded.

But there are other cases where the lines are crystal clear and quite alarming, where New York City APS has fallen demonstrably short of fulfilling its obligations. And those failures have had dire consequences for many desperately needy clients.

These are the cases in which, for whatever reason, APS workers have shown up at a client's door and, having been refused entry, simply walked away, never to return. Or those in which APS has found some legal loophole, enabling it to reject a case that by all rights it should be accepting.

You can read all about APS's cringe-worthy deficiencies in the New York media or hear about them directly from furious tenant advocates, legal aid lawyers, and other social service case managers.

"Cases get forgotten about for months," lamented a Brooklyn housing lawyer, as quoted in a lengthy 2002 newspaper article that depicted New York City APS as a broken, overmatched adversary in the never-ending war against disaster.

"They're just not good for our clients," insisted another tenant lawyer in that same article. "We avoid them like the plague."

Gwen, a long-time family friend and geriatric case manager at a

Manhattan NORC (naturally occurring retirement community), reports having made numerous APS referrals over the years that went nowhere.

"I remember this one case of an elderly client, her daughter and the granddaughter living in this grotesque apartment. Neither her mother nor her grandmother had taught the teenager about feminine hygiene and there were sanitary napkins scattered all over the floor, and a lot of other debris. I referred the grandmother out to APS and when they got to the home, the client wouldn't let them in, so they just turned around, walked away and that was all there was to it....

"I found out later that APS had been in the home before and conducted a few heavy-duty cleanings. I could sympathize with their frustration in having to go back there again and again, and not have anything change, but that doesn't excuse their actions. When you get a new referral, you're supposed to investigate it, no matter how many times you've been there before."

Lori Delagrammatikas of the National APS Association says that such behavior on the part of APS would be wildly improper in all 50 sovereign states.

"The standard protocol in these situations is to make all reasonable efforts to gain entry, through additional home visits or phone contact with the client," she says. "A number of states consider having *seen* [and spoken with] the client, at the front door or at another location, as being sufficient to make a determination as to eligibility."

That was my basic modus operandi: take whatever steps necessary to get through the door, at the client's volition. If gaining the client's permission proved impossible, meet him or her on neutral turf. And, if all those efforts fail to allay concerns about the client's safety in the home, you go for the jugular, in the form of a court order to gain access.

In another more recent case that involved an elderly couple at significant risk in the community, NYC APS was able to weasel out via a highly questionable interpretation of its acceptance criteria.

"The wife and husband could not manage their finances, comply with medical treatment, or take advantage of public benefits," says a social worker familiar with the case. On top of that, she adds, the husband, suffering from mid-stage dementia, had taken to verbally abusing his spouse.

However, the wife had a home health aide in place, and, according to the APS worker who made the initial visit, this constituted having a "responsible adult" on the scene who was able to provide a sufficient level of assistance. As long as the aide remained in the home and the rent was paid up, the worker insisted that neither husband nor wife was at the kind of risk that would warrant APS involvement.

This explanation was a load of hogwash.

The aide, a decent and caring individual, had been performing household chores that were not only well outside her purview, but could potentially get her into very hot water with her employer and law enforcement. These included using the clients' money to pay their essential bills—a big legal no-no for a home attendant—and using her own money to buy the woman food after the husband had run through their monthly food stamp allotment. Aside from that, the wife's aide could do nothing to get the husband to take his daily medications or see his physician.

Nevertheless, all these facts left the APS worker unmoved, and the case was rejected.

Five months later, notes the source, the increasingly demented husband threw his wife out of the house and into the street, causing her subsequent hospitalization.

"And that's as far as we know about the situation," the source says. "Could be they both wound up being placed [in nursing or adult homes].... I can't help thinking it would have all gone so much better for both of them if APS had picked up this case when it was first referred."

That 2002 newspaper exposé of New York City APS further cited a bevy of scandalous failures of the most elemental kind: not filling out proper forms, not making necessary phone calls, or not returning urgent calls. And worse were the cases of workers evincing a stunning lack of empathy toward clients to the point of indifference, if not outright contempt.

One APS worker described in the article was loitering outside a client's building, smoking a cigarette, waiting calmly for the marshal to arrive and conduct an eviction. A kindly, inquisitive neighbor approached, wanting to know if there was anything APS could do at this late date to keep the disabled lady and her three dogs from homelessness.

Not my problem, explained the worker, dismissively. There's no affordable housing in this great big city for a woman and three dogs on a $604-a-month budget, she added.

"Well, can't you do *anything*?" the neighbor asked again. "The woman can barely get down the steps."

"I told her 'Write your Congressman,'" answered the worker. "We're not in the real estate business."

54

Chapter 5. ...And Damned If You Don't

What this worker had to say about the severe shortage of housing for poor people in New York City and APS not being a real estate agency sadly remains all too true two decades later.

Nevertheless, that being said, there is no justification for treating an eviction like a minor annoyance. Here, you clearly had either a once-conscientious worker with a bad case of burn-out, or a worker who should have never been hired in the first place.

Over the past 10 years, since leaving APS, I've worked part-time for a geriatric case management agency, helping seniors get Meals on Wheels, home care, supportive counseling, and other benefits. It's a low-pressure job, and you get to do some good in the world.

As an outsider, I've witnessed the dark side of Adult Protective Services: the unreturned calls, the botched paperwork, and the willingness to give up on cases before exhausting all the options.

But, once again, to be entirely fair, New York City APS is a large bureaucracy within a huge bureaucracy (the Human Resources Administration) within a huger bureaucracy (the City of New York). And bureaucracies of this size tend to be beset with red tape, rigidity, duplication, waste, apathy, customer dissatisfaction, and sluggish decision-making.

Add to all that the fact that APS crisis managers are, like everyone else, flawed human beings, who find themselves buried under mountainous caseloads, uncooperative and out-of-control clients, and fierce pressure from above to wrap up cases promptly and move on to the next.

In such a pressure-cooker environment, mistakes are to be expected—Lord knows, I made my share—and many of the clerical errors and oversights, even the glaring ones, may be excusable, to some degree.

Allow me, then, to put it this way, with further reference to the immortal Bard of Avon. During my years on the job, I never for an instant thought of myself and my colleagues, as "plagues" on our clients' houses.

And for my purposes here, I'll just leave it at that and move on to the next case.

CHAPTER 6

A Crisis Manager
Walks into a Bar...

As you came from the Holy Land of western New York
state, were the graves all right in their brushings/was
there a note of panic in the late August air because the old
man had peed in his pants again....
—John Ashbery, "As You Came from the Holy Land"

Friday afternoons in APS World rarely proceed without a note of panic in the air, even more so in late August, as you're walking out the door with visions of a weekend of fun in the sun. Invariably, this is when the very worst cases are dumped in your lap, or, just as demoralizing, when your previously stable cases suddenly go haywire. In the metaphorical language of the poet, Friday afternoons are when the elderly client who has been continent for more than a year starts peeing his pants again.

But if a crisis manager survives the Friday afternoon curse, he or she is likely to stroll into a friendly neighborhood dispensary of alcoholic beverages, where colleagues are gathered at a table near the end of the bar, talking shop and laughing boisterously.

Just as the bartender has opened the tap and poured out a fresh pitcher of brew, the crisis manager has opened up on another week in the trenches of the down and dirty.

The worker got a new case and sorely needs to share it with the group. As fresh hells go, it is quite the doozy.

The client in question, a middle-aged, heavy-set Caucasian bachelor (SWM), without benefit of a degree in architectural design, had constructed within his one-bedroom apartment a replica of a medieval Italian city. Rather than brick and mortar or wood, his construction material of choice was 25 or 30 years of his own bodily waste—liquid and solid—which he had neatly packaged in hermetically-sealed plastic containers and zip-lock bags and meticulously arranged in byzantine patterns throughout the home.

The soldiers patrolling the gate of his private city were a platoon of rats arrayed along the radiator, guarding the locked fire escape window. There was very little room to move about within the apartment. The client had apparently become rather adept at slithering through the archways and maneuvering along the dark warrens and narrow, winding passages. Presumably, somewhere in the back of the apartment was a place to sleep and something approximating a toilet.

The worker had not attempted to enter the premises, if that were even possible, but had gotten a good look inside through a partially open door. She previously described it to me in colorful language that I will not repeat here.

The next day she brought me along to witness the scene, perhaps because she needed corroboration. It was the kind of sight that once you've seen it, you desperately wish you could un-see it.

I was initially inclined to give the place a name, for in a different, even more perverse world than ours, it might have made for a popular tourist attraction. But, when it came down to it, this tiny slice of purgatory was not worthy of a name. And besides, it was about to be short-lived.

Days later, the cops, having gotten wind of a potential public health emergency, busted through the fire escape window. The rats proved to be unreliable centurions and scurried away as the cops crashed in. The client attempted his escape through the streets, but the police chased him all the way down the block before collaring him and slapping on the cuffs. He was taken to a hospital psychiatric ward and, to the best of my knowledge, subsequently placed in a men's shelter.

As to his girlfriend, who had a senior-level job in a Wall Street brokerage house (so help me, I'm not making this up as I go along)—I have not a clue as to her fate. I do believe it's possible that the client ultimately moved in with her, which could not have helped but be an improvement in his living conditions.

"The girlfriend had to be some kind of fetishist," suggested the caseworker.

With the apartment now vacated, the landlord, bless his crooked little heart, hired a few undocumented immigrant day laborers off the street to come in and clean the place out. They reportedly worked for more than a week in that hellhole without benefit of hazmat suits, face masks, surgical gloves, or any other personal protective equipment. If there is a more revolting way to earn 10 bucks an hour while risking the contraction of typhoid, mercifully I am not aware of it.

Anyway, this was the repellent subject matter of the evening's bar banter. To us, it was surely a strange new variation on the usual "Collyer" story (see Chapter 19). But it was palatable conversation. However, as I looked around me, I couldn't help but notice that to other patrons within earshot, it was not coming off as anywhere near palatable.

One of those patrons approached the bartender and whispered in his ear. The bartender walked over to our table and interrupted the laughter.

"What in hell is wrong with you people?" he said. "Look, if this is what you're gonna be talking about all night, you're gonna have to take it outside. Far outside."

We weren't so far gone as to be oblivious to his concern for his other customers. Respectfully, and to avoid getting the bum's rush, we toned down the volume and kept the discussion fit for normal human consumption.

Over the course of my tenure at APS, I can recall other such occasions, in other bars in other parts of the city, where a bartender's intervention was required. At such times I wished that like cops and firefighters, APS workers had bars they could call their own, where these tales could be told out loud, without shame and retaliation.

Pool tables, dartboards, and Guinness on tap—all that would be nice, too.

Anyway, the program director, who was well-versed in abnormal psychology, in the aftermath of the above-cited case, provided a clinical perspective. The client, according to the boss, was suffering from a rare psychiatric disorder stemming from very poor toilet-training. The result was a total inability on the part of the adult client to part with anything that had once been a part of himself. A city of excrement was his solution to this conundrum.

It all sounded entirely plausible to this layman, but I needed some amplification for the book. I turned all the way to the other side of the globe, to Nick Haslam, one of the world's foremost authorities on the far-reaching impact of bad childhood bathroom behavior on adult functionality.

Haslam, a professor of psychology at Melbourne University in Australia, is the author of *Psychology in the Bathroom*, a wickedly naughty and surprisingly entertaining exegesis on a very qualmish subject.

"WOW!" responded Haslam in an email. "That is a spectacular case!"

I had expected Haslam, who describes his preoccupation with bathroom psychology as a "hobby" rather than a vocation, to concur that the problem with this client had originated at the toilet seat.

But the Aussie threw me a curve.

"It sounds a lot more like hoarding [than fetishism], unless there was a sexual component you didn't mention," he wrote. "There's also a total lack of insight, combined with an intense unwillingness to let go of possessions." (Once again, turn to Chapter 19 for an in-depth discussion of the hoarding phenomenon.)

"It doesn't ring true that someone who carefully packages his feces had poor or no toilet training. He presumably had adequate bowel control, just did weird things with the products.

"So I guess as much as I'm left in awe of this case," Haslam added, "I see it as not very different in kind from someone who holds onto every newspaper and builds maze-like piles of them around the apartment until social services get involved."

While I had the professor's attention, I ran by him a couple of other old cases that involved elderly female clients using their bathtubs as fecal storage units. Here, the ubiquitous toilet came right back into play.

"I'm reminded by a case where the woman was so bothered by the idea of dirtying the toilet bowl that she hid her feces. I think these cases are less about retaining something than hiding away something disgusting, perhaps associated with a delusion [like the fear of a toilet or a desire to keep it unsoiled]. It's clear that there is some paradoxical attempt to maintain tidiness and order by sequestering feces in one place.

"But," concluded Professor Haslam, "no doubt there's something very unhinged going on."

Unhinged.

An apt word, I thought, encompassing much of the APS experience, from the bathroom to the barroom.

APS Versus APS

In the Marx Brothers film, *Monkey Business*, there's a delightful comic riff in which Groucho attempts to sell bodyguard services to a gangster by explaining that he will not only defend the gangster against other gangsters, but he will attack him as well. Two services for the price of one. There's no way to do full justice to Groucho's inspired lunacy on the printed page, nor, I suppose, will I be doing full justice to the following nuthouse tale of APS.

But here goes....

Client number one was a 69-year-old man who picked up a much younger woman (by 20 or more years) and brought her home for a one-night stand. Apparently, it went pretty well, at least for the man, as the evening frolic morphed into a two-night stand, and then a three-night stand. Eventually, the stand expanded all the way to 30 nights, which is where our little tale of woe begins. In New York City, once a person has resided in a certain habitat for at least 30 days, he or she is entitled to "squatter's rights." These grant to the squatter the right to not be evicted without a legal order from a housing court judge.

So once the woman in question had managed to hang in there for the required 30-day period, she had obtained for herself a quasi-permanent residence. According to the former APS worker who related this story to me over a plate of Pad Thai, the woman was a grifter and a seasoned pro at the classic squatter's rights scam. The poor senior citizen, after 30 joy-filled nights in the sack, never knew what hit him. Now, he had a roommate he couldn't stomach and couldn't shake, and with whom he could no longer do what he'd been doing for the first 30 nights of their relationship.

Fortunately for him, he possessed sufficient wherewithal to summon APS for assistance in evicting her. The worker came from an independent, non-profit agency retained by New York City's Human Resources Administration to provide contractual APS services.

Chapter 7. APS Versus APS

As for client number two in our little comedy of errors, that would, of course, be the squatter herself.

Once the man had initiated the requisite action in housing court, the woman turned to APS for help in fighting the eviction. She was assigned her own crisis manager directly from New York City's own in-house Adult Protective Services unit.

So here it was, more or less straight out of the lunatic mouth of Groucho—APS, attacking and defending two clients, simultaneously.

Well, as I heard it, the dueling APS workers performed their jobs adroitly and strictly by the book. They arranged for both clients to be psychiatrically evaluated and assigned guardian ad litems to represent their individual interests in housing court. What then transpired in the courtroom were nine enervating months of grinding legal maneuvers: motions, adjournments, more motions, and assorted other mindless delays.

It was determined that there was ultimately only one way for APS to satisfy the conflicting needs of the two clients: find appropriate housing for the woman, so the poor man could get his home back, and the squatter did not have to go into the street and back on the squat. But, as I noted earlier, locating affordable housing in any of the five boroughs of New York—especially housing suitable to penniless APS clients—is about as difficult as finding Jimmy Hoffa's body or a convention of leprechauns.

Meanwhile, the two ex-lovers and now arch-enemies were forced to hole up together for the better part of the year in an apartment barely big enough for one person. *What must that have been like?* I thought to myself, letting my imagination take over.

The woman, who, as stated, was an old hand at this game, was poised to better weather the situation, whereas her roommate, who had to spend every waking minute of every day with the stranger who had crushed his romantic fantasy and otherwise ruined his life, would be having a much tougher time of it.

I thought of the two of them carefully side-stepping each other in that tiny apartment, battling over everything, from control of the TV remote to who bought the container of chicken salad in the refrigerator. I thought of the two harried APS workers, making their monthly home visits at the same time, trying their darnedest to maintain what must have been a very tenuous truce. And then it occurred to me that maybe this story is not all that different from those of some unhappily married people I've known over the years. The major difference here being that

61

most unhappy marriages don't get mediated by multiple APS workers and legal guardians.

Anyway, at long last, APS managed to find a new home for the woman in a subsidized rental apartment building. They also assisted the client in obtaining Social Security income sufficient to afford the new place. Once she had officially moved out of the man's apartment, the warring APS cases were closed.

The woman, now secure in her new home, was free to move on to a more lucrative grift. As for the man, he reportedly ended up okay, too, albeit after recovering from a bad case of Post-Traumatic Stress Disorder. I'm sure his recovery was hastened by once again having established total control over the remote.

I further suspect that, henceforth, the male client became a lot more circumspect about how far to extend his one-night stands.

CHAPTER 8

In Harm's Way

When in danger or in doubt, run in circles, scream and shout.

—Herman Wouk

When it comes to serious threats to life and limb, my stay at APS was a fortunate one. I recall but two perilous incidents: one pretty scary, the other pretty funny.

The scary one first.

The client was a 20-year-old schizophrenic male, living with his mentally ill brother and a set of parents who modeled their parenting behavior on a Grimm's fairy tale. Their two-bedroom apartment in Manhattan had a little something for both cineastes and lovers of great literature, being an odious amalgam of the serial killer's basement in *The Silence of the Lambs* and Miss Havisham's house in *Great Expectations.*

I entered the dwelling the first time at the client's invitation—his folks were not at home and would never have countenanced my presence—and surveyed the place while dodging cobwebs and insect larvae cascading from the ceiling.

The client had stopped attending his day program, where he received psychiatric medication, talk therapy, and participation in various social activities. His refusal to accept those critical services, coupled with the sheer horror of his living situation, necessitated the APS referral.

The client, as you might expect, refused our services, as well. Based on his severe, persistent mental illness, I received an Article 81 guardianship recommendation from the evaluating psychiatrist and initiated that process.

I so advised the family of my plan while we all stood in the courtyard of their building. Suffice it to say that all four considered this course of action an unforgivable intrusion on their lives and were seething with rage. Out of the corner of my eye, I could see the client's brother working his way toward spontaneous combustion, before the brawny young man started coming at me with a ferocious scowl and his fists tightly clenched, ready to pound me into garden mulch.

My pugilistic background was, and remains, limited. Nevertheless, I'd been in a few scrapes over the years and have always found the best course of action for a non-brawler in a street fight with a bigger assailant is to get low, establish leverage, and hopefully bring your opponent to the ground. Once the two of you are wrestling around on the turf, it's likely that onlookers will move in and break up the melee.

So I got low to the ground, set my feet, and prayed for deliverance.

It came in human form.

Only a few feet from my face, the brother's case manager, a big fellow himself, lunged in front of his client and put a halt to the madness. For this act of kindness toward a fellow case manager, I rewarded him with my sincerest thanks and a glass of very good brandy.

On the day of the guardianship hearing in Supreme Court, I was advised that rather than allow their son to have a legal guardian, the family had chosen to pack up and move lock-stock-and-barrel to Kentucky. It was the first and only time in my social services career that I had driven a client clear out of town.

The second episode of violence—or near-violence—occurred on a home visit to a financial management client whose compliance with her psych medications was sketchy, at best. The client was a short, stocky lady with a quirky disposition, more quirky than usual on this particular visit.

For whatever reason, the client declined repeated requests to sign for her money. She knew I could not disburse it without a signature, but she just kept flat-out refusing. I tried to reason with her for 15 minutes and then got up to leave.

"I'll come back with your money when I get a chance," I said, "but I can't promise when that will be."

Before I got to the door, the client let out an ungodly scream and leaped on my back, wrapping her legs around my waist and her arms across my chest. I stumbled a few steps before instinctively throwing out my left elbow and nailing the client right in the solar plexus; a move seen regularly on *World Wrestling Federation Smack-Downs.*

The lady went flying backward, landing with a thud against the back of the living room sofa.

It took a moment or two to gather my thoughts, as I'd never before assaulted a client, let alone a female one.

64

Chapter 8. In Harm's Way

"Are you okay?" I asked her. "My God, what got into you?"

The client looked up at me and damned if she didn't start laughing.

Apparently, the blow to the chest cavity was just the jolt she needed to transition from violent-and-crazy to peaceful-and-sane.

I couldn't help but share in her laughter. It must have been quite a sight, the two of us sitting on the couch laughing hysterically.

"I'm really sorry about all this," she apologized. "Can I please sign for my money now?"

With most clients, I'd have been concerned about having an assault complaint lodged against me. But this was a client who clearly appreciated the psychological benefit of engaging in a bit of Wrestlemania with her case manager.

I'm happy to report that further interactions with this client went a lot smoother.

Among all my colleagues, incidents of actual violence on the part of clients were exceedingly rare, which should not surprise those with intimate knowledge of mental illness. As for their immediate families or collaterals, however, it was another story.

After one female APS worker in the Bronx gained access to the client's home via an OGA, she and the accompanying psychiatrist discovered a mother and two daughters—a severely developmentally-disabled daughter was the client—living in a sparsely-furnished apartment.

"It reminded me of some of the homes I saw when I practiced in Appalachia," says the psychiatrist. "Dirt floors, bare, stripped of all possessions."

The client, for her part, was unable to communicate at all, and the mother, for whatever reason, was likewise unable to provide any meaningful information. The other daughter—the "dominant" figure in the family who had been refusing entry to the APS worker and was reported by the referral source to be "belligerent"—was fully cooperative with the psychiatrist's interview. There were no signs or indications that the client was being abused or neglected by her mother or sister. Things were going so serenely, in fact, that when the two cops on the security detail requested permission to depart before the visit had concluded, the psychiatrist gave the okay.

However, once the visit was over and the psychiatrist had exited the door, she turned to witness the dominant sister pummeling the horror-stricken APS worker, who sustained minor bruises in the attack.

"I had no choice but to call 911," recalls the psychiatrist, "and because they couldn't take the [assailant] out of the home without endangering the lives of the other two family members, all three of them had to be taken to the hospital."

The belligerent sister was shortly released from the ER, and the APS worker declined to press charges. As there was no evidence found of abuse, neglect, or other major risk factors such as hoarding or eviction, it is likely that APS went ahead and closed the case.

Nevertheless, there were ramifications in the wake of this unfortunate episode. A somewhat-chastened NYPD management henceforth declared that its officers could no longer leave the scene of an OGA until the home visit was completed, and social services had left the building.

On another joint visit to conduct an evaluation on a client deemed "undesirable" by his landlord, the psychiatrist remembers feeling comforted by the size of the APS worker, who, at six feet and 250 pounds, gave the psychiatrist some feeling of security, a security that turned out to be elusive.

Before the interview started, says the doctor, the client went dashing out of the apartment, only to return with two other guys, one claiming to be his lawyer and the other an unremarkable-looking fellow who said very little.

"The guy who identified himself as the lawyer takes my hand and won't let go, and drags me into the kitchen," recalls the psychiatrist. "It was weird enough just having to do my first-ever psych evaluation with a client's lawyer present, and this so-called lawyer is presenting as pretty strange.

"I interview the client in the kitchen, and there's something not right about him, either. I'm not sure after talking to him that he's actually living in this apartment, or subletting it temporarily, or whatever. He's telling me his upstairs neighbor is following him around all day, and he's expressing some weird paranoid ideations.

"I finish the interview and me and the APS worker get up to leave and the lawyer has locked us in the apartment, telling us we can't go until I let him speak with a 'city lawyer,' whatever that is. I'm realizing that this lawyer, whether or not he actually is a lawyer, is truly nuts, and now I'm feeling like we might be in real danger here. We're on the second floor, and I'm looking toward the window to see if we might be able to get out that way.

"Finally, the client himself walks over and opens the door to us. And the lawyer says, 'If you let these two out, I'm not going to be your lawyer anymore!' Anyway, we got out of there and didn't look back."

An episode more fraught with danger featured an elderly client who was not paying his rent, living with a son who had some big-time anger-management issues. The young man had recently been paroled from federal prison following a lengthy stretch for drug-dealing.

It was very clear to the worker that the son presented a risk to the client, who spoke in hushed tones so as not to be overheard by his son in the next room. The case manager voiced her concerns to the boss about the client's safety and her own. The boss was dutifully sympathetic but still sent her back into the home for the psychiatric evaluation.

"So, me and the psychiatrist are in the apartment, and the psychiatrist says he'd like to have a few words with the son, who's lying on the couch. He walks over and asks if he might speak with him for just a moment. The son looks up at the shrink, and glares at him. The kid had menace written all over.

"'If I were you,' he says to the doctor, 'I would get the f—k out of here before I blow your head off.' It sure sounded to me like he meant it."

The psychiatrist, clearly shaken, nevertheless walked back to the client, completed his evaluation and he and the APS worker departed without further ado.

Back at the office, the case manager had some choice words for the boss.

"I'll be damned if I'm going back there again to have my life threatened," she said. Her male colleagues chimed in, in full support of her position.

The boss's response was to assign a couple of male workers to go back to the home.

"And, at this point, every man on the staff stood up and refused," remembers the worker. "'You can't be asking us to risk our lives,'" they said, in unison.

Turns out that a third home visit was unnecessary. The next contact APS had with the client was at the hospital, where he had been taken after his son, in a rage, slashed his father's throat ear-to-ear and put a fist through one of his eyes.

The client declined to press charges—no surprise—but an APS supervisor reported the incident to law enforcement. The son's parole was revoked and he was returned to prison to serve out the remainder of his term.

Once the non-payment issue was resolved, the client was deemed safe in his home and his APS case closed, presumably to be re-opened years later upon the son's release from the slammer.

Adding a touch of vinegar to the client's singularly bitter family life—remember what Tolstoy said about unhappy families—his two daughters held their father solely accountable for sending their misunderstood brother back to prison and cut off all contact with their old man.

Short of actual, or threatened, physical violence, females on the job regularly encountered male clients whose behaviors left them feeling uneasy at best, and frightened at worst.

"On this job, you need to develop a sixth sense about danger," says Leslie, a retired APS case manager. "I had one middle-aged guy, who was generally okay, until one time we're sitting at his kitchen table and there's this look in his eyes I hadn't seen before. He starts licking his lips and leering at me. The whole thing didn't feel right.... I just got up, gave some excuse, and left."

Teresa, a former worker in Queens, recalls a similarly unsettling experience with an elderly client in Far Rockaway.

"He was this tiny man who'd just gotten discharged from the hospital after a hernia operation. He kept saying he wanted to take off his pants and show me his surgical scar, and little by little, I'm beginning to feel a kind of sexual tension that's really creeping me out ... then, as I remember, the two of us walked into the kitchen and he tells me he's got a beautiful collection of knives and would I like to see them. At that point, I'd seen and heard enough to tell me it was time to depart.... I grabbed my bag and got the hell out of there fast."

Teresa's advice to all the women who dare to venture into these mannish domains:

"Always be near a door, and always let your gut be your guide."

CHAPTER 9

That Guy Who Looks Like Felix

My ex-wife and I had this silly little game we used to play.

After committing some venial household sin, like leaving pie crumbs all over the kitchen counter, silverware in the sink, and my clothes strewn about in every room in the apartment, I'd invariably deny having done it.

"I see," the ex would say. "I guess it must have been that guy who looks like you."

"Yes," I would reply. "It was the guy who looks like me. He's around all the time, screwing up everything."

That-Guy-Who-Looks-Like-Me became a long-running gag in our 16-year relationship and occasionally crops up in arguments with my current spouse.

My old client, Felix, played silly games like that: silly, annoying, aggravating little games.

Felix was a sweet-tempered but rascally young man with a tremendous aversion to opening his rent bill and an even deeper fear of losing control of his finances.

When I first got the case, I obtained a one-shot deal for Felix to pay off his arrears, contingent on our becoming his representative payee and assuming responsibility for his monthly rent payments going forward. Felix did not raise any fuss about it, maintaining his warm and friendly demeanor toward APS. He just took a casual stroll over to his local Social Security office, explained to some novice clerk that it was all a big mistake and requested that he be reinstated as the recipient of record.

And the Social Security clerk, without bothering to check into this matter or contact anyone at APS, simply complied.

I think you can see where this story is going.

I had to once again go through the rigmarole of putting the client back on financial management and straightening things out with the New York City Housing Authority, which had a strong aversion of its own to rent scofflaws.

And, once I'd put the procedure back in place, Felix, with a smile and a shoeshine, sashayed back to Social Security, found another clueless clerk behind the counter, and had the whole process reversed yet again.

And then again.

I can't recall precisely how many times Felix overturned APS Financial Management during the time I had his case, but it was often enough to drive his case worker batty.

Of course, our office reached out to Social Security a number of times. What was the purpose, we inquired, of gaining control of a client's monthly check in order to keep him safely in his home, if said client can simply walk into your office and undo everything we accomplished with just a few pleading words?

"We understand," the Social Security functionary would say. "We'll look into it."

And then Felix would return to their office and once again turn everything topsy-turvy.

When I took up the matter with Felix himself, he denied responsibility. *It wasn't me*, he said. *I can't understand why this keeps happening.*

"It must have been that guy who looks like you," I suggested to Felix.

"Yes, that must be it," he replied, with a big grin. "It must be tough on you, having to deal with someone like that."

CHAPTER 10

The Two Faces of Esther

Well, who are you?
—Pete Townsend

Esther was a single, slender, and rather mousy Jewish female in her late 50s or early 60s, who lived alone in an expansive split-level house in Northwest Queens that was bequeathed to her by her wealthy parents. Her only regular companionship was provided by a housekeeper and an impressive collection of stuffed animals.

She had referred herself to Adult Protective Services.

She told the intake worker over the phone that she was being "stalked, harassed, and exploited by a Hispanic man in my neighborhood."

"He opens up credit cards in my name," continued Esther, "and he goes through my mail and steals it. I call the police all the time but they keep ignoring me. Finally they told me to call APS."

When Maria, the crisis manager, first arrived at the scene, she found a client with a shiner on her right eye and in a heightened state of anxiety.

Esther reiterated, in a high, squeaky voice, what she'd said at the intake about being threatened and financially exploited, adding a new allegation of felonious assault, as evidenced by the black eye. But to her case manager, meeting her for the first time, the story didn't seem to add up.

"I couldn't quite put my finger on it, but there was something really amiss here," says Maria.

Skepticism in matters like these is an unfortunate, but unavoidable hazard among veteran APS case managers. Female clients—for want of attention, acute paranoia, or any number of psychological reasons—frequently report threats and violence from male neighbors and acquaintances that prove to be unfounded and sometimes imaginary.

I recall one client who insisted that a New York City police officer

71

who lived next door was climbing into her bedroom window every night and waking her up to watch him furrow through her underwear drawer, try on every pair of her panties, and select the one he would wear back to his place. I did some checking and found no active or retired NYPD personnel living nearby—the next-door neighbor in question was an elderly widow with her own collection of lingerie, who said the client had been driving the whole neighborhood crazy for years.

Maria made two or three subsequent visits to Esther's home over the next couple of weeks, and on each one, she became more suspicious about what was really going on.

On Maria's last visit, the client added to the list of alleged misdeeds, claiming the perpetrator had broken into the house a few nights before and raped her. This also appeared to fail the smell test, as the client's house had been equipped with the latest and greatest in-home security technology. But, according to Esther, she had solid, incriminating evidence. The rapist had left behind a blood-stained sports jacket.

"Okay," said Maria, "now we actually have something we can show the cops. Could you please go upstairs and fetch the jacket?"

Esther quickly returned with the evidence. Upon examining the jacket, Maria gently asked the client to put it on.

It fit her perfectly.

"I could see before she tried it on that there was no way that little jacket would fit a grown man," says Maria. "It was clearly the client's jacket."

So, as far as the rape allegation was concerned, it could be persuasively argued in court by a defendant's lawyer that if the clothing fit, one must acquit.

But all this didn't answer the larger question of what was actually going on in the house.

That is, until Esther uttered the first words after putting on the jacket.

"I nearly crawled out of my skin," recalls Maria. "What came out of that mouth wasn't Esther's tiny voice. It was a loud, masculine voice. Like a voice in a horror movie, like the devil's voice coming out of little Linda Blair in *The Exorcist*."

"Little bitch!" the voice bellowed. "Yeah, I did her! And then I tripped her up and knocked her all the way down the stairs. Little bitch deserved it.... HAHAHA."

To Maria, this was something out of the mind of Rod Serling—specifically the *Twilight Zone* episode in which a derelict finds a dead gangster's loafers in the trash and assumes the gangster's personality when he slides them on.

Only this wasn't television, and the transition was happening right in front of Maria.

"At this point, I'm in a full state of panic," she says. "I'm thinking this poor woman is going completely psycho on me. So, I slowly edge my way toward the front door to get the hell out of there before she becomes physically violent."

And then, Maria had one of those epiphanies, familiar to APS case managers and Spanish mystic poets.

"Suddenly, the whole thing just came together in my head and began to make sense. I had it figured out."

It wasn't the client herself who was talking in a man's voice. It was a separate and distinct male personality who had been sharing space inside the body of Esther. The putting on of the sports jacket was the trigger that prompted the appearance of the Hispanic male perpetrator. Not an imaginary figure. A real, living presence in the household.

"Multiple Personality Disorder" is what this was called back in Rod Serling's day. Now its formal name is "Dissociative Identity Disorder," characterized by two or more personalities inhabiting the same individual, often as a reaction to a trauma from a distant past. The condition is quite rare. There are said to be fewer than 200,000 active cases in the U.S. There is no cure, but experts say psychotherapy, or "talk therapy," is the main prescribed treatment and has been helpful in many cases. (See Joanne Woodward successfully treat Sally Field in *Sybil*.)

Other therapeutic modalities have achieved moderate success, including the aforementioned Cognitive-Behavioral Therapy, EMDR (eye movement desensitization and reprocessing) and Dialectical-Behavior Therapy (geared to people with the most severe personality disturbances from abuse or trauma).

The ultimate aim of all these therapies is to "reconnect" the various personalities into one integrated, well-functioning identity. Again, I highly recommend *Sybil*—the TV movie or the book—for those interested in the subject.

But enough of the abnormal psychology lesson.

Maria, now armed with the truth, began putting the remaining pieces of the puzzle together. The black eye had, indeed, been inflicted by a man. The client, it seems, had been venturing out at night to testosterone-fueled bars around town, in the personality of, and dressed as, her male half. He was a male with an intemperate disposition that could result in barroom brawling, for which his unimposing physical stature was ill-suited. Hence, the shiner and blood stain on the jacket he/she had worn to the bar that evening.

"The police had the full picture for a long time," says Maria. "And all they could ultimately do was recommend to the client that she get some serious therapy, which Esther had absolutely refused to even consider. So the cops just stopped responding to her calls."

Another curious aspect of this case was an allegation from Esther's female self that her housekeeper, a Caribbean woman in her late 20s or 30s, was stealing her money. Esther advised her case manager that she was extremely well-off in that regard, but that didn't mitigate the fact that the housekeeper had finagled considerable cash from her over the years.

Maria followed APS protocol in putting through a referral for a psychiatric evaluation. The visiting shrink, however, was not privy on his visit to the emergence of the Hispanic male. In the absence of a second personality, he deemed the client to possess capacity and to present no danger to herself/himself or others.

The housekeeper, it turns out, was not the most virtuous of characters—she had been charging the client $1,000 for her company over the weekend—but there was no evidence of extortion, and the client ultimately admitted to willingly overpaying her aide just to have someone to be with on Saturday nights. That is, at least on those Saturday nights when he/she wasn't hitting the dive bars.

"I remember the housekeeper telling me that she'd been getting a huge kick out of watching the client being two-people-in-one," says Maria. "She thought this whole multiple personality thing was hysterically funny."

Maria remembers the case as the opposite of funny.

"Very scary, very sad ... and very APS."

CHAPTER 11

If I Had a Rich Man

In the midst of chaos, there is also opportunity.
—Sun Tzu

We've all read obituaries of prominent people and after reading them, muttered to ourselves, "Now, *that* was a person I would have liked to have known in life."

Such was my reaction upon reading the *New York Times* obituary of Perry Hoffman, dated December 3, 2019.

I had never heard of Dr. Hoffman, a former elementary school teacher turned social worker, turned Ph.D. Had I known of this kindly and gentle woman while I was working at Adult Protective Services, my tenure there would most likely have been less draining and irritating.

Hoffman in the 1990s and early 2000s—about the time I was taking up APS work—was conducting ground-breaking research into Borderline Personality Disorder (BPD), an all-to-common psychological condition that has afflicted patients and their social service providers for generations. It most certainly afflicted me, as I had a great many borderline cases over the years.

I remember leaving one such client after a psych evaluation circa 2004 or '05, and bitching to the psychiatrist that I could no longer abide these life-sucking people.

The shrink shook his head and laughed.

"Make me a list of your 20 most exasperating clients," he said, "and I will guarantee you that 17 or 18 are diagnosed borderlines."

At that time, there was no known cure for this disorder, and, even worse, no effective treatment. It was Perry Hoffman who helped break down that wall.

The DSM-5, the desk reference guide that elucidates and classifies all identifiable mental disorders, defines borderline personality disorder as follows: "A pervasive pattern of instability of interpersonal relationships, self-image and affects, and marked impulsivity beginning in early adulthood."

Characteristic behaviors include "frantic efforts to avoid real or imagined abandonment"; self-damaging impulses (binge eating, substance abuse, overspending , etc.); recurrent suicidal gestures or threats, or self-mutilation; intense mood swings that may last as long as a few days; chronic feelings of emptiness; difficulty controlling frequent displays of anger and recurrent physical fights; and stress-related paranoia.

Moreover, people with BPD often think in extremes, a tendency known as "dichotomous," or black-and-white thinking. In this scenario, situations are either perfect or horrible, with nothing in-between. One's friends, family members or social service workers might be the greatest people in the world on one day, and the most contemptible, hateful creatures the next.

On paper, all these criteria can come off as dry as the vermouth blowing a kiss at the gin. But let me assure you that out here in the fields of dysfunction, nobody can raise your hackles or your blood pressure faster than a borderline in full throttle.

What used to get to me worst of all were those precipitous 180-degree mood swings, so swift and unpredictable, and the rapid-fire switching from benevolent gratitude to wrathful loathing.

My first hard-core borderline—I'll call him Marvin because Marvin is a name that suits him well—was a true test of patience and fortitude. He was a man of many mood swings and a proclivity for black-and-white thinking.

But apart from all that, Marvin was a virtuoso of the dark arts of manipulation, a skill likewise highly common among borderlines; he knew instinctively and precisely where all my psychic buttons were located, almost as if he'd sewn them on himself. And he knew how and when to press them to unleash my inner demons and eventually get his needs met. A maven of manipulation was my Marvin.

The client, who referred himself to APS, was living in his own apartment in Brooklyn, driving a cab part-time, and making just enough money to slow his rate of starvation. I got the client a one-shot deal to cover his rental arrears, and convinced a close relative to guarantee future rent payments. I also obtained Medicaid health care coverage and food stamps for Marvin. All through these processes, he was calling me just about every day, usually asking why they were taking so long and questioning what kind of nincompoop he had representing his interests.

Chapter 11. If I Had a Rich Man

When all the issues were satisfactorily resolved, Marvin turned quickly into my Best Friend Forever.

"How can I ever thank you?" he gushed.

And gushed, and gushed.

And then came the inevitable day not long after when I failed to reauthorize Marvin's Medicaid, and he temporarily lost his health coverage. I apologized for the error and assured Marvin that I had taken the proper steps to have his health insurance reinstated quickly.

But Marvin's mood had swung too far to the wrath to turn back. He reacted as though I had just driven a monster truck into his living room.

I don't remember all the colorful expressions Marvin employed on that call, but I do recall the outburst going on for quite some time and revealing Marvin's innate talent for profanity and calumny. Like a dentist's drill, Marvin's stinging words bored into the thin protective covering of my self-esteem, exposing every tiny splinter of self-doubt.

While this diatribe failed to completely shatter my self-worth, I admit to being unnerved. I took these deep feelings of unease to the boss for assuaging.

Being neither my wife nor my mother, he did not offer a warm shoulder, just some good, sound advice.

"The borderlines will do that to you," he said. "You will have to find your own way of taking their reactions in stride, or you won't be able to function here."

And, of course, over time, I made considerable progress on that score. The borderlines still aggravated the daylights out of me, but Marvin was the first, and last, borderline to mount even a moderately successful, full frontal attack on my delicate ego.

Months after I'd closed Marvin's case and moved on to the next borderline, I had the misfortune of bumping into him on the subway. His emotional pendulum had by this time swung all the way back to BFF. But, strangely enough, I didn't care for Marvin as my buddy any more than I did as my nemesis. I felt that if I happened to say the wrong thing, the pendulum could very well swing back again, resulting in a final demoralizing encounter, this one on a public conveyance.

So I shook Marvin's hand, wished him the very best, and got off a few stops shy of my destination to wait for a Marvin-less train.

When Dr. Hoffman first began her research into BPD, it was commonly believed in psychiatric circles that hostile, critical family environments exacerbated its symptoms. But Hoffman discovered quite the opposite; it was overprotective, doting parents who caused the most damage.

The story of Ruthie, the 50-ish daughter of a wealthy and permissive widow, supports Hoffman's original thesis.

Ruthie lived all alone, and lonely, in a luxury high-rise cooperative apartment purchased for her by her mother, who had been keeping Ruthie above water since childhood. Ruthie treated her apartment shabbily, as she did her person, and both mother and landlord were concerned that her hoarding problem and self-neglectful hygiene were getting out of hand.

Nevertheless, by hoarder standards, Ruthie was a minor-leaguer, and her apartment didn't rise to anywhere near an eviction-level nuisance. Ruthie, herself, was something of a nuisance, but they don't necessarily evict people in this town for being hard to stomach.

"I don't know what to do with my daughter anymore," lamented her aging mother, who had made the APS referral as a last gasp at salvation.

"I just give her money and more money, and nothing changes. She keeps coming back for more. And she does nothing all day, nothing but sit in her apartment and cry to me on the phone that her life is horrible, and it's all my fault."

I had a number of discussions with mom about her enabling behaviors, and she was savvy enough to recognize her culpability in keeping her daughter chained to dependency. But mom had her emotional needs, too, and weaning her off these controlling behaviors was well outside my scope of practice.

As for Ruthie, she was, without doubt, the most self-sabotaging individual I'd ever met. She wasn't angry or malicious in the manner of Marvin, but so set in her paranoid ideations, abandonment fears, and extreme thinking, that she was incapable of taking any action to improve her life. Even worse, she was incapable of even envisioning such action.

One day, we sat in a little public square outside her building and talked about her future.

"Do you know where I can go to meet a rich guy?" she asked. "That's what I need, a rich man, someone who'll take care of me."

Ruthie said she had once had a rich boyfriend, and he bought her a lot of expensive stuff that made her feel safe and secure. It was 30 or more years ago, back when Ruthie was young and lovely and may have had some faint hopes of escaping her mother's pervasive influence.

"I wish I could help you," I said. "But we're not matchmakers at APS."

Nevertheless, this was the first time Ruthie had mentioned having a goal of any kind, and even one as tenuous, if not insoluble, as a rich boyfriend, may have represented a baby step forward.

I attempted to draw her into a casual discussion of what initial actions could be taken to potentially attract a gentleman of means, like cleaning her apartment, bathing, doing her laundry on a regular basis, and finding something to engage her mind and spirit—volunteer work or a part-time job, for example. Little steps on the long road to personhood.

Ruthie had a bevy of reasons for not being able to accomplish any of those things. It was a sort of sick game we played out there on the street. Me, making a suggestion; she, shooting it down as unworkable; me, suggesting an alternative strategy; she, shooting it down for other reasons; and on and on like that into the late afternoon, finally ending up right where we'd started: with Ruthie bemoaning her pathetic life, and blaming it on her mother, and every man she's ever known, including yours truly.

Ruthie lived perpetually in what psychologists refer to as a mental "loop" that goes 'round and 'round and always returns to base camp: the utter impossibility of change.

"So, let me ask you again," concluded Ruthie. "How can I meet a rich guy?"

Today, according to mental health professionals, the most severe cases of borderline personality, like those of Marvin and Ruthie, are now routinely being treated successfully via a variety of therapeutic modalities.

One reported to be especially effective is Dialectical Behavior Therapy, as mentioned in the previous chapter.

The "dialectical" refers to the bringing together of two "opposites"— acceptance and change—as a means of validating the client's experience and using it toward the development of a whole new set of interpersonal skills. DBT patients are given "homework" in the form of daily diary cards on which they track their emotions, urges and behaviors.

Perry Hoffman, for her part, helped pioneer the use of DBT for BPD, but, perhaps most important, she developed "Family Connections," a 12-week program under which the families of borderline patients meet in groups and teach each other how to cope, under the guidance of experienced therapists. That program is now being employed throughout the world and has become a virtual model for other mental health support organizations.

"He probably won't shoot you"

I stand in awe of those who have led the fight against this infernal, tenacious disorder. I liken these BPD pioneers to Louis Pasteur, Tensing and Hillary, and the Birdman of Alcatraz; those intrepid individuals who have battled impossible odds to bring humankind to a higher plane of existence.

On behalf of current APS workers across this great land of ours, I salute you.

CHAPTER 12

Naked Came the Stranger

Unflappable. Unruffled. Composed.

Adjectives that well described Asia, an APS crisis manager with whom I worked in Manhattan. She was an experienced worker and had seen quite a lot in her time.

But when Mr. Hernandez opened his apartment door to let her in, Asia saw more than she bargained for. Mr. Hernandez stood calmly and unabashedly in the doorway, naked as the day he was born.

At that time, APS unwritten guidelines concerning interactions with clients who were nude, or otherwise putting their unmentionables on display, generally recommended that the worker, prior to entering the domicile, do his or her best to convince the client to cover up. Preferably in clothing, but barring that, in a bathrobe, a beach towel or a blanket. Should the client decline repeated requests, the worker was advised to back off and attempt a second visit at a later date. Should that visit yield the same result, then the next step was to return with a supervisor. In no case was a worker to engage in a frank and lengthy dialogue with a client in a full state of undress.

Asia pondered this option, and, concluding that the fastest and easiest path between two points is a straight line, decided to go forward with the assessment, the client's indecorous behavior notwithstanding.

She made sure to position herself as far from the client, and as close to the door, as the apartment layout allowed. Apart from his appearance, Mr. H. was fully cooperative with the interview, which went off without a hitch. I think it would be safe to assume here that the two parted without a handshake.

When Asia returned to the office, she reported all this to her supervisor, as the client's disdain for sartorial matters was a relevant fact in the case. She explained that, in her best judgment, the client did not present as a sex fiend or garden-variety pervert. She simply wanted to get the job done, and she appeared to be entirely comfortable with that decision.

Her supervisor, who related this story to me, was nonplussed. But he trusted in Asia's judgment, and suggested that in the future she be less cavalier when encountering such situations.

Field workers, especially female ones, were a lot less understanding of Asia's thought process.

"That was, without doubt, one of the stupidest things I've ever heard a worker do," says another former APS crisis manager. "You should never put yourself in that kind of danger. I don't care if the guy seems as nice as Andy Griffith and sits 40 feet away. Naked is where you draw the line."

As for me, I never had a client, male or female, come to the door in a birthday suit. And that's a little sad, in a way, because I had the perfect Borscht Belt punchline all set up for the occasion:

"Hey, my wife's got an outfit just like that!"

Still, I did have clients over the years whose inappropriate modes of dress created tension. One middle-aged female client, whose objection to covering the lower half of her body was matched only by her objection to paying her rent on time, presented a sticky problem.

My solution was to bring along a female colleague on my home visits. This worker developed a nice connection with my client, who was self-medicating daily with vodka and orange juice. My colleague would gently wrangle with her for a few minutes at the start of the visit, but would always manage to get her into a pair of pants. And once she was sufficiently covered, we could get down to the important business of keeping her from being evicted and getting her on some proper, prescription medication.

With male clients of a similar immodest nature, I was much more comfortable. Here, like Asia, I'd settle for long distances and imagine that the client was fully dressed—the very opposite of what they tell you to imagine when you're nervous performing in front of an audience of strangers.

One last curious, but unsurprising, note:

I found it to be almost axiomatic that a client's tendency to go topless or bottomless was inversely proportional to the client's physical attractiveness.

Which is, as by now I'm sure you are all acutely aware, totally on-brand at APS.

CHAPTER 13

Rules of Engagement

Here are some basic, commonsensical tips for today's Adult Protective Services case manager. You will not find these suggestions in any manual, but they are just as important to one's job survival as anything in the guidebook.

- Be nice. If the client curses you out, calls your mother's honor into question, disparages your intelligence and competence, or denigrates your religion or ethnicity, be nice. Address the clients as Mr., Mrs., Miss, or Ms. To quote Patrick Swayze in *Road House*, one of the most gloriously godawful movies ever made, "Be nice ... until it's time not to be nice." In my experience, that would be when a client's very large and very schizophrenic older brother attempts to turn you into his personal hand puppet.

- Develop a thick skin. A wise man once said that APS is the one social services endeavor in which, whatever the outcome of a case—good, bad, or indifferent—there'll be somebody out there who isn't happy with it. Or with you. You could rescue an entire family from homelessness, feed a hungry mouth, or even save a life. Nevertheless, you can be fairly certain that a sibling, cousin, nephew, or some other friend or family member will accuse you of violating the client's rights by putting him or her in the hospital or gaining control of the client's money. I once had a client with late-stage dementia who, along with his family, was facing eviction after he had been peeing all over his apartment, the building hallways, the laundry room, and the courtyard. We put a stop to the eviction proceeding by having the apartment cleaned and lightly fumigated and putting a legal guardian in place who eventually had the client transferred to one of the best nursing homes in the state specializing in the care of dementia patients. His daughter, who lived somewhere out in the suburbs and had up to this point done little or nothing to address her

83

father's situation, called me out of the blue and accused me of just being in it to gain control of her father's Social Security money. On the phone, I reacted with courtesy and restraint. "I'm sorry you feel that way," I said. "Would you like to take this matter up with my supervisor?" Like I just said, be nice.

- Be creative. In a time of extremely limited government resources to address seemingly intractable problems, it becomes necessary to look for help in places you may not have imagined existed. For example, in the aforementioned case of the serially incontinent client, all that urinary output had penetrated so deeply into the walls, floors and furniture of the cooperative apartment that a pervasive, noxious odor had rendered the home unsellable—at any price. I did some online research on removing stubborn urine smells and found a company that, for a surprisingly modest fee, would truck in heavy vacuum equipment to suction the lingering odors out of the most rock-solid surfaces. The family, being tight-fisted in the extreme and having become accustomed to even the worst smells, didn't want to spend the money. Nevertheless, I left behind the business's contact information, should they ever decide to sell the property or give their tortured nostrils a break.
- NEVER, EVER, leave your briefcase, handbag, or any other kind of carry-on baggage on the floor of a client's home. There may be creatures abounding, and you don't want to be opening up your bag in your own living room to find a pair of cockroaches mating, or worse, one of those aforementioned Norwegian sewer rats attempting a repatriation to Norway. I learned this particular lesson the hard way. My wife found it necessary theretofore to remind me that if I ever again brought one of these nasty varmints back into our household, I should consider myself to be in need of a divorce attorney.
- In that same vein, when in the client's home, avoid sitting in thickly upholstered chairs or sofas where insects may be lying in wait for a new posterior upon which to alight. If possible, plant yourself in a less comfortable, but less bug-hospitable plastic or metal chair. By the way, contrary to myth, bedbugs don't fly and are not hard to spot. But there are other kinds of vermin that lie in cushy places and can't be seen by the naked eye. And they, too, will get you in serious trouble should they happen to accompany you home.

Chapter 13. Rules of Engagement

- And, finally, while we're on this entomological track, it's important to throw in a few more words about bedbugs, because you will encounter them quite often on the job and, as your great-grandparents used to recite when putting your grandparents to bed, you don't want to let them bite. In my years at APS, I found it necessary to don a hazmat suit only three or four times, and only in homes that were infested with this scourge from floor to ceiling. In this work, building trust with clients is more essential than in any other field of social services. You will find that task tough enough—especially in an age where social distancing has become a social imperative—even when you aren't reenacting the emergence of Neil Armstrong from *Apollo 11*. I tended to err on the incautious side in most bedbug infestation cases, but this is one calculation you will have to make for yourself.

- Make friends with your dry cleaner. If you're spending prolonged periods—15 or 20 minutes can be considered prolonged—in certain homes that exude highly unpleasant odors, you will doubtless bring those odors back with you to the office or the home front. With all this new business and a little friendly banter, the dry cleaner might be inclined to give you a volume discount. And, along those same lines, rethink all you've been taught about dressing for success. In this line of work, that generally means dressing down to fit the occasion. Not necessarily all the way down to the client's level, but enough that you won't stand out and look ridiculous. Once, I went out on a home visit prior to attending an evening performance at the Metropolitan Opera, dressed in a blue suit. It was off the rack, but I never felt like such a tool.

- Do not eat or drink anything offered by a client, unless it comes out of a vacuum-sealed container or an unopened bottle or can. It's not that I don't believe that most clients can be gracious hosts or hostesses. It's just that ... well, my trusting nature doesn't extend far enough to swallow a client's fresh-baked, chocolate-walnut brownie. A former colleague of mine, heretofore a firm adherent to this particular code of conduct, recalls letting her guard down just once and accepting a glass of tap water from a client. What she didn't know was that the tap water had been stored for some time in a filthy metal jar in the refrigerator. "I never knew a glass of water could taste so foul," she said.

• Avoid, if at all possible, using a client's bathroom, especially if you happen to be on the distaff side. "I never would even think of asking clients to use their facilities," says a former APS female worker. "But when you gotta go, you gotta go, and this was one time when I had no choice. The bathroom was pretty clean, thank God, so that part was okay. Anyway, there I am on the bowl doing my business, and I suddenly hear a little voice behind me. 'Peek-a-boo, I can see you,' it says. I start to freak out. Turns out it was the client's eight-year-old grandson taking a bath, looking at me with my pants down to my ankles through the curtain. So, yeah, going forward I'd use a filling station restroom rather than go through something like that again."

• Do your assessments as near to an exit—front or back door, ground-floor window, or fire escape—as possible. Do not blithely walk through a door with a barking dog on the other side. Through the door, simply request that the client remove the animal to a closed room. I happen to love dogs, but many dogs who live with severe, persistent mentally ill (SPMI) clients have a way of taking on the immoderate characteristics of their masters.

• Trust your gut. Don't wait until the client's 6'5", currently off-his-meds schizoaffective son threatens to bash in your brains. If your instincts tell you that there is danger afoot, get the hell out of there ASAP.

• Never believe your referral (see introduction). As often as not, the people and situations you will encounter on your initial assessment visits will bear little or no relation to what is described on the referral sheet. Expect the unexpected. The most ghastly-looking, cadaverous clients will amaze you with the energy and intensity required to fill a three-bedroom split-level with rubbish. And, conversely, the most vivacious clients can be the most bereft of spirit. Human behavior is always a mystery. At APS, it's a mystery, wrapped in a puzzle, with a ribbon of enigma.

• Do not hesitate to ask for backup on a home visit. If you're of the African American persuasion and the client is an Aryan supremacist, or you're a young female worker with a Hasidic Jewish male client, it might help to bring along a lily-white colleague or a yarmulke-wearing associate. Moreover, if there's a hint of potential danger in the referral, I have found the local precincts to be amenable to offering police escort. Once upon a home visit, a pair of very scary gangbanging drug dealers, who had taken over an elderly client's apartment in the projects in Far Rockaway, opened the door to me. I was mighty glad to have had two of New York's Finest by my side. The two drug dealers, not so much. And that holds true when dealing with "EDPs," police shorthand for emotionally disturbed persons. When, during another home visit, a floridly psychotic client in Queens tried to dig her way from her living room floor all the way to China with a hammer and shovel, I was grateful for the presence and the support of a few burly cops.

- Criminals and crazies aren't the only people who may be prone to intimidating you on the job. The APS quality assurance workers who audit your files can have a similar effect when it comes to evaluating your job performance. Don't let them get under your skin. One worker I know warned in a final case note that the person taking over one of her most difficult cases— that of a developmentally-disabled man living in an apartment with a drug-dealing brother—should be careful not to enter the premises while the deals were in progress. The worker got written up for not immediately calling the cops. "I told the auditor, 'If I ratted out the drug gang, I could no longer make visits without my life being in danger. It's not an ideal situation in there, for sure, but the brother is not abusing the client, and the client now has Medicaid Home Care in place and all his basic needs met.... I made the right call.'" Upshot: after a little back-and-forth, the auditor agreed and backed down off her high horse.

- Getting back to the subject of gangbanging drug dealers in the projects or in high-crime areas in general: it is wise to make your home visits the very first thing in the morning, particularly if you're carrying a few thousand dollars of FMU cash. Criminals tend to be night people and rarely awake before noon. You'd do best to be out of there when they emerge into the light. It's another lesson I had to learn the hard way. Once, in the dead of a New York winter, when the sun sets before 5 p.m., I made a late afternoon visit to a wheelchair-bound grandmother in the Brooklyn projects who was allegedly being physically abused by her junkie grandson. When I got there, the gangbangers (Crips, judging from their colors) were out in force on every stairwell, shooting craps or just hanging out. I was extremely fortunate that they let me pass without incident. But it was pitch black outside by the time I had completed my initial visit, and I did not relish a nighttime walk down four flights of Crips-controlled stairs (the elevator being busted). Nevertheless, I lucked out once again, managing to slip-slide away unnoticed and unharmed.

- Should you find yourself confronted by hostile forces on a home visit, there are a couple of tips that might help you get through it. First, do not ignore a gang member who addresses you directly. However, you might view this snub, it will most definitely be taken as disrespectful, and nobody hates being disrespected more than gang members. Better to simply tell them what you're doing on their turf. Criminals have mothers and grandmothers, too. And just like other people's mothers and grandmothers, they are sometimes in considerable need of Medicaid home care, food stamps and heavy-duty cleanings. A mugger might find it unseemly to rob someone who's there to help his aged grandma remain safely in her community.

- Always be off to the side when knocking on a client's door. This I learned from a city marshal who narrowly missed being struck by rifle shots fired through a wooden door. Understand that some people distrust and fear Adult Protective Services almost as much as they do the cops. And some of those people are armed.

- Watch out for the kiddies. The Fourth Amendment might curtail your efforts to assist your recalcitrant clients, but all bets are off when it's children in the home who may be abused and/or neglected. Reporting these cases is mandatory for all social service agencies, but, even if it weren't, this is a moral imperative. I'm thinking here of one particularly egregious case of an elderly client living in a narrow studio with her emotionally disturbed daughter and her even more disturbed granddaughter. The conditions under which they were living were deplorable, but that was the least of it. It seems the granddaughter kept bringing young men into the apartment for sex, which was okay in itself, except she rarely used birth control and was blessed—or cursed—with the fertility of a fruit fly. It was an FMU case, so it dragged on for years, through the multiple impregnations, abdominal bloating, ice cream binging, and ultimately, to the birthing of a great many unwanted babies. And, as per the ongoing APS referrals to the Administration for Children's

Services, there was always an ACS representative on hand just outside the delivery room to snatch the baby away and give it a fighting chance at a decent life. There was nothing APS could do, of course, to stop a young woman from procreating, but we could damn well do something to protect our nation's future.

- And, in that vein of standing up for the truly helpless, I would refer you to Proverbs 12:10, which affirms the righteousness of caring for our animal friends. You will likely find more animal abuse and/or neglect on the job than you will endangered children. As one who once lived among four finicky cats, three super-friendly Labrador Retrievers and a teenaged boy, I implore you, when you witness such cases, to drop a dime to your local ASPCA. It's the Biblical thing to do.

- Don't attempt to go it alone. Rely on your colleagues and supervisors for support, concrete and otherwise. Many of the cases you'll come up against are complicated and fraught with potential perils, physical and emotional. Some will test your patience, some your sanity. And some may make a grown man or woman weep. Whether the vehicle is regularly scheduled peer review meetings, or Friday night get-togethers in the local pub, don't be shy about sharing your feelings with your workmates. They've all been where you are, and their insights and empathy will be invaluable.

- Nevertheless, while your colleagues may be the only ones who genuinely understand what you're going through, it helps enormously to have a significant other, or others, with broad shoulders and the ability to "listen with the third ear." A former worker laments that when things were at their worst on the job, she was married to a guy too wrapped up in his own problems to care about hers. Her advice: "Find yourself someone you can talk to about cockroaches and bathtubs full of excrement."

- I used to tell my elderly clients that the keys to a long and happy life are to keep moving and keep laughing. I don't have to tell you to keep moving—the job will do that for you. But laughter, in the field of Adult Protective Services, is a cleansing agent the likes of which there is no other. And it's a gift of which you must constantly remind yourself, because most of your cases will be most unfunny. You've got to find your own path to the laughter because it will not easily find you. You have to be able to find it in an old man's allergy to his pants (think Homer Simpson),

or a client's effort to keep you in her apartment by climbing
on your back and wringing your neck (think World Wrestling
Federation). You have to find the laughter even in that proverbial
bathtub full of excrement, perhaps most of all in a bathtub full
of excrement. The alternatives to this kind of laughter—trust
me on this—are sleepless nights or finding a more pleasant
way of earning a living. And one final thought on laughter: it's
infectious, contagious to your colleagues and supervisors. Laugh
in an APS office, as they say, and you'll never laugh alone. "They
gave us our own floor to keep us away from the other social
service departments," says the former director of a big-city
APS unit. "And every day the people on the other floors would
complain about the noise, the laughter and the pranks we pulled
on the rest of the building. There really was no way to explain to
outsiders how necessary laughing is to the functioning of an APS
operation."

• Familiarize yourself with the term, "countertransference" (as
referenced in Chapter 1). It is most often used to describe a
common occurrence in psychotherapeutic environments, but it
applies equally to those doing non-clinical social service work.
If you can't find your way clear of becoming enmeshed in the
lives of your clients, you will be useless as a case manager. On the
other hand—at APS there is always another hand—countering
countertransference can be a danger in itself, if it causes you to
back off a case too much and too soon. One of my strengths, and
weaknesses, as a case manager was a tendency to work my cases
aggressively and hold on to them for too long. Hell, what was
I doing in a thankless job like this if I wasn't willing to spin my
wheels like a trucker hip-deep in Mississippi mud? I don't regret
that oft-wasted effort, as the effort can be its own reward. I guess
I'm just saying, once again, that APS is no place to work if you
aren't getting your hands dirty and your arms sore from tilting at
those infernal windmills.

• Unless you've earned a Master's in social work, try not to
describe yourself as a "social worker," especially in the presence
of those with advanced degrees. It may seem petty to you,
because you're working side by side with social workers
and performing the same basic functions. But I've known
credentialed social workers who take poorly to having non-
credentialed workers overstate their qualifications. I tend to

think of it this way: as a former emergency medical technician, I know how to take vitals, administer oxygen, staunch an arterial bleed, and deliver a baby in the back of an ambulance. None of that makes me a doctor.

- Avoid situations that might create liability issues for you and your APS organization, or, equally important, uncomfortable feelings for you. One fairly common circumstance on an initial home visit is a client who insists on being interviewed in, or partially in, the buff (see the previous chapter). If said client wishes APS services, it should not be a problem getting him or her out of a birthday suit and into a bathrobe, beach towel, or, best of all, a shirt and slacks. But should the client remain adamant about remaining naked, it is highly prudent to bid a hasty retreat.

- And, lastly, heed the words and wisdom of the late Gambler, Mr. Kenny Rogers: "Know when to walk away, know when to run." To my mind, APS crisis management has to be more than a means of making your rent payments and putting food on your table. It doesn't have to be a Heavenly Calling or a Great Adventure, but once you find yourself jaded to the point where you're in it just for the paycheck and the occasional laugh, do yourself and your clients a favor and fold your cards.

How Do You Solve
a Problem Like Tobias?

In this world, you must be oh so smart, or oh so pleasant.
Well, for years I was smart. I recommend pleasant.
— Elwood P. Dowd

There is a tendency among APS crisis managers to compartmentalize. When you have a caseload exceeding 40, and growing at an alarming clip, this is a natural defense to an impossible situation. Like, say, gallows humor, or vodka straight up.

"What do you need?" asked one former colleague, to whom I had reached out for input on this book. "I can give you eviction cases, elder abuse, hoarding, physical violence. Give me a category; I'll give you a case."

But what of those clients, few as they might be, who defy categorization? Who exist in a realm outside human dysfunction, going their own way, breathing their own rarified air. Once upon a caseload, I was assigned one of these singular individuals.

Allow me to introduce you to Tobias.

He was a tall, awkward Caucasian of indeterminate age, who had emigrated to the U.S. from somewhere in eastern or central Europe as a young man. His history was a mystery. He had been, at least for a brief period, some kind of engineer in the old country, but beyond that, the record was blank. Tobias had no family there or here. He'd never married or had children. He had no belongings, aside from a few changes of clothes, a pair of brown loafers without heels, bed linens, a clock-radio, and a rusty bicycle.

Tobias said very little, and when he did speak it was with a very rapid cadence and in barely audible tones. At first, I thought this stemmed from a lack of English skills, but it was more like Tobias just didn't have all that much to say that he hadn't said long ago. What Tobias did like to do a lot was smile. Pretty much all the time, actually.

Chapter 14. How Do You Solve a Problem Like Tobias?

Over the two-plus years I had his case, I came to see Tobias as a spiritual cousin of Elwood P. Dowd, the genial, engagingly wacky protagonist of the Pulitzer Prize-winning play, *Harvey*, about a dipsomaniac whose best friend was a 6-foot talking rabbit, audible and visible only to Elwood. No matter the chaos swirling around him, Elwood was always smiling, happy with what life had dealt him in the moment.

Tobias didn't need an invisible rabbit friend, although I'm sure he would have embraced one. Everybody in his Brooklyn neighborhood was his friend. And if they weren't his friend, but were merely exploiting his warm and trusting nature, it didn't matter to Tobias. A monthly visit from an APS worker, rarely a joyous occasion in any client's life, was to Tobias one of life's manifold simple pleasures. One might say that every day was a beautiful day in Mr. Tobias's neighborhood.

At the time of the initial APS referral back in 2004 or 2005, Tobias was living in a deteriorated multi-family Victorian dwelling, made considerably more rickety by a lack of routine maintenance. The owner had sliced and diced up the interior to accommodate 15 or more small bedrooms on three floors, most of them occupied by adult males very far down on their luck. Now the landlord, for whom Tobias had only good thoughts, was in the process of selling the house, and all the residents of this patently illegal single-room occupancy (SRO) residence were being forced to vacate the premises.

The referral for Tobias came from one of his neighbors, who had more or less been looking out for him for years. As a veteran of New York City's labyrinthine social service system, Tobias's housemate knew the ropes well enough to help his friend obtain SSI (Supplemental Security Income) and Medicaid healthcare insurance benefits. But relocating Tobias to new affordable housing was a task well outside his scope of expertise.

I put through an immediate request for a psych evaluation, which could help buy Tobias some time in housing court and would be necessary in relocating him to an adult living facility that would accept his benefits.

Silly me.

The first psychiatrist who attempted to evaluate Tobias was as confused and clueless as I. I recall she concluded that at some time in his young life, Tobias must have been severely traumatized. But in what way, and to what effect, the psychiatrist was at a complete and total loss. Leaving Tobias's room, she turned to me and shook her head.

"There are some clients who make you throw up your hands and

93

surrender," the psychiatrist said. "I wouldn't know where to begin with this guy."

Nevertheless, the shrink was somehow able to come up with a serviceable rationale for a diagnosis of mental disability, which would be helpful in our efforts to assist the client moving forward.

Soon after, I brought Tobias to a clean and reputable adult home, not far from his former digs, to be interviewed for a coveted placement. I'd built a good relationship with the admissions director of the home, having already placed several clients there, most of whom had adapted well to their new surroundings.

The director was taken by Tobias's affable demeanor and didn't press him too hard for personal details. On my strong recommendation and Tobias's having passed the physical and the TB test, his application for a shared room was accepted. It came with three hot meals a day and other onsite services. The ground rules for residents were minimal: no drinking or drugs; notify management when you're leaving the building for any significant length of time; and respect your fellow residents. Otherwise, Tobias would be free to live his life, unencumbered by the rigid strictures typical of nursing homes and most assisted living facilities.

I moved Tobias into his new home on a Monday afternoon.

He didn't make it to Tuesday.

"He slept here maybe half the night at most," recounted the residence manager. "Then he took off to I don't know where."

I soon located Tobias back at the old house, in his old room. He offered no explanation. I knew then that any housing or other standard-issue solution that I could muster would never for a moment accommodate the needs of Tobias.

Ultimately, he stayed on as the sole remaining occupant of the SRO. We set him up with financial management in order to ensure prompt payment of rent to the new landlord. But the new owner, for whatever reason, elected not to charge Tobias any rent or utilities. So, every month I would deliver to Tobias the entire amount of his SSI check—approximately $700–in cash. I usually found him in a neighborhood diner, where the proprietor, another old friend, fed Tobias three square a day and gave him a safe place to hang out. His friend also bought him some new clothes, toilet articles and a pair of shoes with heels, all in return for Tobias sweeping up the place throughout the day and keeping an eye out for mice.

The owner told me that Tobias had no need for the money I was handing him. Free cash was as disposable, and meaningless, in his daily life as it would be to an eccentric billionaire. He gave it away to anybody and everybody, even those without a plausible sob story. Petty grifters and muggers in the area had a field day with Tobias, the easiest mark in the Naked City. The diner owner said Tobias usually disbursed his entire monthly allowance before the first week was out.

Thereafter, in response, I held back a portion of Tobias's money, which I gave to the owner for safekeeping in the event the client might need it down the line. This was admittedly a violation of APS rules governing the dispensing of financial management (FMU) cash, but it was a corner I felt comfortable cutting.

As long as FMU was in place, I made my regular visits to deliver the money and touch base with one of my favorite clients. Nothing changed as the months wore on. But, eventually, Tobias exhibited symptoms of what could have been a respiratory problem. And, in true Tobias fashion, he was refusing to see a doctor.

The diner owner, who looked upon Tobias as a sort of surrogate offspring, graciously agreed to become his legal guardian, which would bestow on the owner the authority to compel Tobias's compliance with medical treatment. With APS' imprimatur, and Tobias's approval, the guardianship application was accepted, and I closed the case.

In point of fact, I did little or nothing over the course of two years to advance the cause of Tobias. Indeed, my major accomplishment was getting as far out of the way as possible and letting the man live his life as he saw fit.

Every now and then, I bump into Tobias on the street—where nobody hustles him anymore—or in the diner, where he feels a sense of belonging. Many nights, he sleeps on a cot in the rear of the restaurant. As far as I know, he still has a bed back at the old house, if and when he chooses to lay his body down there.

"Mark," he says whenever he sees me, "I miss you, my friend."

He gives me a smile and a hug and tells me that he's doing just fine and dandy. No worries, mate. Nothing here to see but a man who wakes up each morning, grabs a mop, a pail and a hot cup of coffee, and welcomes the new day like the miracle it is.

Every case should end half so well.

Tender Mercies

*I've learned that people will forget what you said, people
will forget what you did, but people will never forget how
you made them feel.*
　　　　　　　　　　　　　　　　—Maya Angelou

He was looking for God too high up and too far away.
　　　　—Spencer Tracy, in *Inherit the Wind*

Judge Bronstein, a Queens housing court magistrate with an
easy-going and warm bench-side manner, addressed my client as we
stood before him.

The judge patiently tried to explain to the man that if he continued
to refuse APS services, he was virtually guaranteeing his own eviction.
He became frustrated when the client, although fully intact mentally,
did not seem to understand or care about his predicament.

Then the judge turned to me for a little ex parte communication.

"With all due respect, I have to ask you this," he said, sotto voce.
"Why the f—k would anybody in his right mind do what you do?"

I would illuminate the why thusly:

Back in the mid–1980s, my mom, dad, and I went to say our
final farewells to a dear family friend who was in hospice care for her
late-stage pancreatic cancer. The IV painkillers were having, at most, a
mild salutary effect. Discussion among our group was difficult, as you
might imagine, but we did our best to hang in there and support our
friend and her husband in their darkest hour.

Then my dad, instinctively, began telling a joke: a shaggy-dog
Borscht Belt story. The old man loved telling jokes and, for an amateur,
he was extremely good at it. Nevertheless, I was skeptical about whether
this was the proper forum for dad to unleash his inner Jackie Mason.

The joke was an ancient one, one you may well have heard before.

Two guys on safari in Africa are seized by a native tribe.

Chapter 15. Tender Mercies

"You have two options," says the tribal chief. "Death or Chee-Chee."

The first guy, naturally, selects Chee-Chee. He is then pulled into the center of the ring and slowly and mercilessly torn to shreds by wild animals, to the deafening cheers of the crowd. Hours later, when he has finally succumbed to this unspeakable torture, the chief turns to the other guy.

"So, my friend, what will it be? Death or Chee-Chee?"

"Are you kidding?" the guy responds. "After what I just saw, I'll take death."

"Then death it will be," pronounces the chief.

"But first, Chee-Chee!"

Our friend, from the depths of her pain, let loose a belly laugh, and we all joined in. The joke had hit precisely the right note of levity, sending a shot of uninhibited glee into the gloom, and allowing my family the emotional space to share our feelings and say goodbye to a loved one as we had envisioned. And, as an added bonus, I remember never feeling so proud of my old man.

On our way home, I thought about how a last laugh, a last sunrise, or a million other seemingly trifling things, can mean a great deal to people at the end of their tether.

When I got to APS 20 years later, I began to truly recognize the enormous value in all those insignificancies on an almost daily basis.

For example, there was Virginia, a new client, who was facing eviction from her small one-bedroom rental apartment. The house had been sold and the new owner wanted all the tenants out so he could renovate the whole place and eventually bring in his own family. Virginia had no lease and was paying rent on a month-to-month basis. Therefore, she had no viable legal recourse.

However, she did have a powerful non-legal defense. A long-time alcoholic, she was dying from cirrhosis of the liver and was already receiving in-home hospice care. Her nurse told me her life expectancy was no more than six to 12 months, and most likely closer to three. No housing court judge I knew of, no matter which side of the bed he or she woke up on, was going to order a sick and dying, wheelchair-bound woman into the streets of Bensonhurst, Brooklyn.

And even if so ordered by a soulless judge, I had it in mind to summon the tabloid press to witness the eviction proceeding. I could not come close to imagining any landlord, even one with the flintiest of human feeling, wanting his children to see a headshot of daddy on the front page of the New York Post, alongside a photo of an enfeebled woman being wheeled out of her home to die like a dog.

No, I didn't see any problem with this case. And, indeed, the guardian ad litem we obtained for the client quickly negotiated a deal allowing her to stay in her apartment for the remainder of her life.

I was ready to close her case and move on, until the client motioned me to her bedside and made of me one last request. It seems her only child, a son, was being held at the jail on Riker's Island following his guilty plea to the charge of beating some other guy half to death in a fight over a woman. The son was awaiting imminent transfer to an upstate New York prison where he would be incarcerated for a term of 1 to 3 years.

"Can you help me to see my son one last time, just so I can say goodbye?" was the client's plea.

While this sort of good deed generally falls somewhat outside a crisis manager's purview, this was a request I could not in good conscience refuse.

So I set about trying to arrange a mother-and-child reunion in proximate time. However, this proved to be no mean feat. New York City and State Corrections Department rules, at least at that time, mandated that visitors could not meet with inmates outside of official premises—a jailhouse or courthouse, for example.

I made an appointment to bring the client to the jailhouse and cleared it with one of the Riker's Island chaplains. But when we arrived at the parking lot, after a bumpy, tortuous cab ride, the guard informed us that the absent-minded chaplain had neglected to notify anyone of the visit, and therefore we were denied access to the facility. The long drive to Riker's had already exhausted the client, and I feared this trauma could actually hasten her demise.

We got her home very late in the afternoon, anguished and frustrated, but still breathing. There was no way going forward that I was going to again subject the client to that kind of emotional and physical stress.

I began reaching out to various officials to see if I could get the rule on family visits waived in this extreme case. I wrote to Senator Hillary Clinton, the client's congresswoman, her state senator and assemblyman, her city councilman, and just about everyone else in government I could think of who might have some pull with Corrections Department higher-ups.

For weeks, I got nowhere with anyone in authority, and time was running out for mother and son. (I should add here that for the son, William, I wouldn't have given party favors; this was solely about granting a dying mother's last wish.)

Anyway, just as I was ready to give up this quixotic quest, I got a call from a source inside Riker's. She served in some sort of social service capacity there. Someone had apparently passed one of my missives along to her, and she was surprisingly sympathetic for a prison employee. Before hanging up, she told me she would do everything in her power to facilitate a meeting.

Days later, I was strolling back to the office from a client visit, when I picked up a voicemail on my cellphone. It was the client, delivering a message that I will not soon forget.

"Mark, it's Virginia," she said. "It's amazing! I saw William last night! I'm so happy I can barely speak...."

She explained that two Corrections officers had, without prior notification, escorted William to her home around 11 p.m. They got the client out of bed and for an hour or so, she and her son spoke quietly at the kitchen table. There was laughter and much weeping, as the two said their final goodbyes.

The officers took pains to cover William's shackles with a blanket. Although Virginia couldn't help but notice the shackles, she was deeply grateful to the officers for that small act of kindness. Up to this night, indecency was about all the prison system had to offer her.

"I said goodbye to my little boy," concluded Virginia. "And it was all because of you. I will never forget what you did for me and William. God bless you."

I found a bench, sat down, and cried. I thought about my dad, who had passed away only a couple of months earlier, after stroking out in rehab. By the time I arrived at the hospital, he was beyond a last laugh, but I made sure that for the 24 hours he existed in a comatose state, he had on a set of headphones playing a Cole Porter/George Gershwin mixtape.

Back at HQ, I barged into the director's office. I was past caring about office etiquette.

"If there was ever a day you wanted to dump a mountain of s—t on me, today's that day," I announced with a flourish. "No matter how awful it is, it's not going to faze me at all. There is nothing anyone can do to me today that's going to spoil my mood."

For on this one blessed day, I was the king of crisis managers. And, as all Mel Brooks fans know, it's good to be king.

"He probably won't shoot you"

Anyway, a week or so later, I paid my monthly visit to Virginia. No one answered the door. I peeked through the living room window, and saw that the apartment had been cleaned out. I walked around outside the building for a while looking for someone to provide answers, until I bumped into the handyman.

"The lady died a few days ago, and they took everything out," he said, confirming my strong suspicion.

So, as they say in the medical profession, the operation was a success but the patient died. Only the first part of that statement holds any relevance to me, then or now.

Anita was a 40-ish Latina who lived in a squalid three-bedroom apartment in a Manhattan public housing project. Life had beaten her pretty much to a pulp by the time I entered it as her APS crisis manager. She had not paid her rent for the past few months, and NYCHA had served her a 30-day notice.

The rental arrears were, to put it incredibly mildly, the least of her woes.

First, there were her roommates, who included a creepy older brother, who had been sexually abusing Anita since childhood, and a crazy aunt who spent long days panhandling by the subway entrance and collecting garbage off the streets, which she dutifully brought back to the apartment every night at dusk. There were also her two children, a teenage girl and an 8-year-old boy, both of whom were understandably acting out at school. Rounding out the household, there was Anita's boyfriend and the father of her kids, a polite enough gentleman, but one with no job prospects or the ability to help the mother of his children navigate this existence.

Then, there was the extremely poor condition of the apartment, exacerbated by the aunt's daily garbage collections and nobody in the household having the strength or desire to pick up a mop or a broom.

And, finally, if all that wasn't enough to suck the life out of a woman who had heretofore known nothing but hard times, there were the results of her last oncological workup. Anita had Stage 4 breast cancer. Inoperable and terminal.

A crisis manager approaches a case like Anita's one heartbreak at a time.

Based on her Social Security income, I got the family a one-shot deal to cover a few thousand dollars in arrears. In the time it took to authorize that funding, Anita fell into arrears again, so I went back and got a second, smaller one-shot. We put Anita on financial management, ensuring that the rent would be paid going forward.

We subsequently brought in the crew for the heavy-duty cleaning, which unearthed a working refrigerator and stove beneath several thick layers of crud. I reached out to another agency that not only helped Anita get into appropriate cancer care, but also worked with me to obtain a Family Court order of protection enabling the ouster of the abusive brother. As for the wacky aunt, we managed to get her placed in a reputable adult home.

I don't want to pooh-pooh all this effort, because it was good, honest work, all around.

But what marks this case as worthy of inclusion in this book came on a home visit I made on one hot summer afternoon to deliver the monthly cash allowance from Anita's financial management account. The brother was still in the home at that time, sitting at the kitchen table, eyeing me with a mix of suspicion and contempt. I could barely look back at this slime bag without overwhelming feelings of anger and disgust.

I took Anita into a rear bedroom to attend to the financial transaction out of the brother's watchful gaze. We sat on a soiled mattress, where she took the cash and signed for it. This visit occurred before the HDC, so the only thing stirring in that airless bedroom was the smell of dirty linen and body odor.

I hadn't eaten at all that day, which, combined with the heat and the assault on my senses, caused me to feel woozy.

"Could I trouble you for a glass of water?" I asked, violating my own cardinal rule against ingesting anything proffered by a client.

"Sure," said Anita, who went into the kitchen and returned with a glass of tap water.

After guzzling it down, my head started to clear and I thanked her. At this point, our relationship had slipped into something beyond client and crisis manager: just two ordinary people helping each other make it through another sweltering New York City summer afternoon. Normally, such a shift in roles is not recommended. But, in this instance, I was grateful for the water and the shared humanity.

Anita, in the quiet of that lonely room, began to cry, softly, and rested her head on my shoulder, while I held her hand. We sat like that for 10 or 15 minutes, saying nothing, as there was nothing that needed saying.

I remember Anita walked me to her door and held it for me.

"He probably won't shoot you"

"Are you sure you're okay to get back to your office?" she asked.

"Yes," I said. "Thanks to you."

As the weeks went on, we proceeded with the HDC, the eviction of the brother, and the placement of the aunt. A referral I subsequently made to Child Protective Services on behalf of the kids brought a regular cleaning lady into the home, as well as counselors to help the children deal with their problems at school and cope with the inevitable death of their mother. Happily, the boyfriend, so underappreciated by me, stepped up to the plate for the sake of his children. He and the kids would remain safely in their home after the dust had cleared.

Once again, the final tally: a dying client and a reward for a thirsty case manager that transcended the normal course of events at Adult Protective Services.

The client passed away and was buried while I was on vacation. One of the volunteers who had worked with me in Family Court told me all about it.

"It felt like we were there to say goodbye to a friend," she said.

I knew precisely what she meant.

Attending the funerals of our clients was generally frowned upon by APS management. Aside from that troublesome countertransference thing, we really didn't have a lot of free time during the day to spend reflecting on the dead.

Mr. and Mrs. Ginsburg were notable exceptions.

The childless couple had more or less been adopted into our APS family. They'd been in the system for what seemed like forever, through multiple case workers and multiple travails. We'd all become attached to them, like one is attached to a family pet who chews up the bedroom furniture and attacks the neighbor's kids.

Mr. Ginsburg was a contumacious, cranky old goat, who had a knack for aggravating landlords and case managers. Give Mr. G a reason to complain about something—like a creaky air conditioner or a leaky toilet—and he'd run with it. Their aggrieved landlord would invariably respond in kind, taking whatever passive-aggressive steps he could think of that would compel the Ginsburgs to seek affordable housing elsewhere.

Mrs. G., for her part, was less ornery, but inclined to stick by her husband, even when he was at his most unreasonable. All these two had were each other.

By the time the Ginsburg case reached my desk, the couple had

102

arrived at the end of the road, relocation-wise. Some years prior, they had lost their home—and their money—most likely through very bad financial management. They subsequently went through a horrendous period of homelessness, living for a time in their car, and somehow managing to get their plight publicized in the New York media. The press coverage led to their arrival at APS. As I recall, we assisted them in finding an apartment with a relatively low rent, put them on financial management, paid their essential bills, and mediated their constant squabbles with the landlord.

We were all, in a sense, stuck with each other. The Ginsburgs, the landlord, and APS in a Bermuda Triangle of tumult.

Truth is, I actually liked the clients and they seemed to at least tolerate me, perhaps because we were co-religionists. I came to enjoy my monthly visits to their apartment, which was always clean and tidy. Every visit began with a complaint, sometimes before I had passed through the doorway. The complaints ultimately played out like old vaudeville routines that never lose their antique charm.

The Ginsburgs, although they didn't necessarily act that way, understood that there would be no future home for them if they managed to screw up this one.

And, as fate would have it, it truly was the end of the line for Mr. G. In short order, he got very sick and died.

The staff at APS, supervisors and workers—countertransference concerns be damned—elected to go together to the funeral service. We comprised the majority of the mourners in the chapel and our presence there was undoubtedly of great comfort to the widow. She would not be abandoned by New York City's social safety net in her hour of need.

This was the only client funeral I ever attended in any social service capacity. But being a client's mourner didn't feel at all strange or uncomfortable. It was, after all, just another way of showing up.

On the day Daquan turned 18—the day he became an adult in the eyes of New York State—Child Protective Services turned him over to me for safe-keeping.

Daquan, whose parents were either dead or missing, had been living with his grandmother in a project in Brooklyn. When she died, a distant cousin took him into her apartment in the same complex to live with her large family. But she was strapped for cash herself and couldn't afford to house Daquan without additional income coming into the household.

"He probably won't shoot you"

I escorted Daquan to a hearing at Social Security, where his SSI application was approved, based on a somewhat questionable learning disability. That income, combined with Medicaid and a small amount of food stamps, made Daquan a contributing member of his new family.

The relationship between Daquan and his cousin was not a smooth one—she resented the intrusion—but at least he was no longer seen as a financial burden.

Where this case got interesting was where I discovered that my new client, after 12 years of public schooling, could not read a street sign. He knew a few letters of the alphabet, but couldn't put them together into words, let alone sentences.

The idea of a kid graduating high school without being able to distinguish "Stop" from "Go" struck me at the time as a scathing indictment of what passes for public education in New York City and a dereliction of the system's responsibility to a student who deserved a hell of a lot better.

I lobbied with my supervisor to keep this case open and began accompanying Daquan into Manhattan for free literacy classes. Soon, he got more comfortable traveling into the city by himself, and he began making a little headway in his studies.

By the time I got around to closing Daquan's case, he was getting up to speed with his ABC's and feeling the first whiffs of excitement that we all feel when we discover the awesome power of the written word. The fact that he was 13 or 14 years late to the party was beside the point.

A few years later, I was at a local Social Security office helping a friend navigate that Kafka-esque bureaucracy, when a man I didn't immediately recognize approached me with a smile and his hand out for shaking.

He could see I didn't register his identity.

"It's Daquan, man," he said. "How're you doing?"

He didn't look anything like the boy I knew. His fresh, pubescent face and thin frame had filled out, and he had an air of confidence about him. My man-child client had morphed into a full-grown man.

"It's great to see you," I said. "What've you been up to?"

He told me he had long since moved out of his cousin's apartment and was living with friends. He had a part-time job as an assistant manager of a movie theatre, and he was reading at an 8th- or 9th-grade level. And, as a kicker, he had a knockout of a girlfriend to whom he introduced me.

He was not just any man now. He was an accomplished man, a

104

master of his own fate. And he could sense that I saw all of that in him, which made his pleasure at seeing me again all the more meaningful. He thanked me for my help in getting him on his feet and we parted company.

In truth, I hadn't done that much to make this transition occur. I simply gave a kid a shove in a positive direction, and then, years later, sat back and took in the result.

I do wonder sometimes what Daquan might have become if a legion of teachers hadn't ghosted him for 12 years. But that's too far above my pay grade.

As I remember, my colleagues and I back then didn't talk at all about the primacy of feeling and other such ethereal matters. But that is not to say that they didn't experience similar evanescent moments of joy, leaving behind feelings and memories that have lasted years.

Lewis, a colleague from Brooklyn, recalls an elderly client, a stroke victim in a comatose state, lying on a hospital bed on the verge of death.

"I knew Agnes to be a deeply-religious Catholic, and I knew some of the members of her church peer group," said Lewis. "So I contacted two of them, and told them that Agnes may be in a coma but nevertheless is in great need of the divine mercy prayer. And I informed her priest, who said he'd come in after the peer group ladies had gone.

"So, me and her two friends arrive at her bedside and begin to pray. And I'm telling Agnes, 'Margaret and Frances are here with me, and we're all praying for you.' Meanwhile, the nurse in the room is rolling her eyes, until she sees Agnes open her eyes, sit up in bed and acknowledge our presence before falling back immediately into her coma.

"'I'll see you again,' Margaret says to Agnes as we're leaving, and then she turns to me and adds, 'somewhere.'"

At this point, the priest walked in to administer last rites. As far as Lewis is aware, Agnes never again came out of the coma.

"What the client needed in the moment was to be prayed for, to be saved," concludes her case manager. "I remember my APS supervisor reading my case note and questioning whether I made up the part about the client responding to the prayer, but it did happen just like I wrote.... Divine intervention does happen."

An observation to which I would add, "All the time."

Our problem as human beings is that we rarely see it happen because we're always looking for that divine spark too high up and too far away.

"He probably won't shoot you"

Another colleague from my Brooklyn days recollects a client who had to retire from her job in her mid–40s after receiving a diagnosis of Crohn's Disease, a chronic inflammatory disorder in which the body's immune system attacks the gastrointestinal tract. The disease is painful as all hell and can have a negative impact on life expectancy.

While the client waited anxiously for her Social Security Disability application to be approved—a process that can be as long as it is anxiety-provoking—she fell into $15,000 worth of arrears on her cooperative apartment maintenance and was facing eviction.

Her only son, a combat soldier in Afghanistan, went deep into his pockets to send his mother $6000 from across the seas. It was every cent he had to his name but less than half of what his mom needed to pay off her debt.

With no income coming in and no basis for an emergency grant from New York City, the besieged client and her case manager appeared before a most austere housing court judge.

"Your honor," said the worker, channeling Clarence Darrow in his stirring defense of Leopold and Loeb, "this [eviction] cannot be allowed to occur. It's an outrage, an insult to humanity … my client has a son a half a world away in a combat zone, putting his life on the line for his country every day, worrying not only about being killed, but whether his disabled mother will be tossed out of her home into the street. An eviction would be a travesty of justice."

The presiding judge took only a brief moment to reflect, before rendering his decision.

"You're absolutely correct," he intoned. "This is not who we are as a country. I'm dismissing this case."

It was less the outcome of this case than the sheer feeling of elation at the judge's words, says the worker, "that will be with me forever."

The simple truth is that everything we do for one another counts for something, and the very things we often dismiss as trivial perhaps count most of all, when we're getting down to what really matters.

I don't hesitate to say that without these little mercies—the holding of hands, a mother's last wish, a final prayer for the needful—I wouldn't have spent seven long years of my life at Adult Protective Services, mostly getting hammered on the big stuff.

CHAPTER 16

WORST. CLIENT. EVER.

This one isn't even close.

The hoarders, the borderlines, the pathologically narcissistic, the ornately psychotic, the trustees of modern chemistry: all present different sorts of challenges. But, over time, one can learn to accept and tolerate these clients in a manner that doesn't greatly impinge upon one's peace of mind.

Nevertheless, every once in a long while, you find yourself confronted by a client so disagreeable, so utterly *detestable*, that all you want to do is resolve the case as fast as humanly possible and jump in the shower.

The client I'm referring to, oddly enough, wasn't even mine. The boss had me fill in for her assigned case manager, and my interaction with the client took place over the course of but a single hellacious day.

The boss didn't issue any advance warning about this case. My simple instructions were to transport the client and her boyfriend, by taxi, from their apartment to the nearest Social Security office for a redetermination of her cash benefits, and then put them both in another cab for the ride home. The client had failed to respond to multiple letters from the Social Security Administration to set up the necessary appointment. Should the client once again fail to appear on this final deadline day, her benefits would be terminated. APS's job was to make sure that didn't happen.

I guess the boss thought this was all I needed to know to complete the task. Still, I wished he had provided some additional case history. Specifically, that the client's boyfriend doubled as her pimp, and a not very pleasant pimp at that. The boss might also have mentioned that on the duo's last visit to our office, weeks earlier, the client had been observed in the waiting room performing an act of fellatio on her partner. In short, he might have better prepared me for what I was in for.

The moment I pulled up in the cab, the pimp boyfriend started in on me. Now, keep in mind that this guy had never seen me before in his life, and my sole responsibility on this lovely April morning was getting the two of them to the Social Security office on time.

The pimp began hassling me about why the client had to go through the redetermination process, why Social Security didn't come to their home, and why the client's monthly benefit amount was so low. He complained about having to show up at the office so early in the morning and wanted to know why I didn't have them picked up in a limo.

He went on in this vein throughout the drive to the SS office and in the waiting room, and whenever he took a little break from excoriating me, the client chipped in and did her bit to make my day as miserable as possible. I should add here that their many complaints were registered in loud, obnoxious fashion, and in language befitting a hooker and her pimp.

I wanted so much to reprise a classic line that a friend of mine once employed when a mini-bordello opened for business across the hall from his apartment. My friend knocked on the door and a man answered.

"I think it is time," said my friend, "for the two of us to have a serious man-to-pimp talk."

Anyway, the day creeped along endlessly in the way that all really bad days do, until the client finally got called in for her reevaluation interview. By about 4 p.m., the interview had concluded, and I rang up the cab company to come and take this twisted pair off my hands.

"What, you're not escorting us home?" inquired the pimp.

"No, I have to get back to my office," I replied. "I wish you both the best of luck, and thanks for being so accommodating."

That's three lies in three seconds.

An APS record.

CHAPTER 17

Both Sides Now

MAX BIALYSTOCK: "You miserable wretch! How dare you take the last penny
from a poor man's pocket!"
LANDLORD: "I have to. I'm a landlord."
—From the movie *The Producers*

Shortly after my arrival at APS, the staff was sent off to a lecture delivered by a housing attorney and fierce tenant advocate. This grizzled veteran of 30-plus years of landlord-tenant wars was a character straight out of a Ben Shahn social-realist painting. She was a leftist firebrand who saw landlords as predatory creatures and tenants as their prey. Her lecture detailed all the many legal, quasi-legal, and downright illegal tactics that avaricious landlords use to harass, exploit, threaten, and ultimately evict decent people from their rightful homes.

As a child of the '60s, growing up in a middle-class environment with a mother who'd been a Communist in the '30s, I was loaded for landlord, ready after that spiel to rush out and man the barricades against the evils of the real estate industry.

And then, something inside me changed. That something was APS.

The client was a middle-aged, working-class Albanian immigrant with a wife and a couple of teenaged kids. The family lived in a 1st–floor apartment in a large rental building. They were being evicted for what was alleged to be some extremely bad behavior.

For openers, the father and son were disposing of the family garbage outside their kitchen window. They both had also been observed on numerous occasions urinating out the bathroom window (you'd know why if you'd seen the toilet). In similar fashion, the old man had also been seen a few times defecating beside the building. The apartment, as you might expect from people with such hygienic habits, was nidorous, feculent, and infested with all kinds of vermin—roaches, houseflies, mice, rats, and Lord knows what else. On my initial visit, I could swear I saw a deceased opossum in the laundry hamper, but it might have been my fevered brain in overdrive.

The APS referral, which as I recall came from the client himself, arrived very late in the process. The family had already received a "marshal's notice," signaling that the day of eviction was imminent. I did what I could. I ordered up an immediate psych evaluation in hopes of having the paterfamilias designated as mentally impaired, so that a guardian ad litem could be appointed to represent him (and by extension, his family) in housing court.

Having met this family, browsed their apartment, and seen the voluminous legal evidence arrayed against them, there would be no way on God's earth to keep these folks in their present home. At best, I had hoped that our legal maneuver would drag out the case for a while to enable us to relocate the family to another apartment. (I can guess what you're all thinking; good luck with that.)

But the judge at the hearing wasn't buying our GAL gambit. The psych evaluation apparently did not make a strong enough case for a mental defect, and the eviction date was now set in stone.

On the day of, as required by APS rules, I accompanied the city marshal to the home, my role there being to provide emotional support to the client and ensure that he was fully advised of all his tenant rights (i.e., the landlord is required to store all the tenant's belongings for at least 30 days before discarding them). Finally, I was there to offer the family free transport to wherever they wished to be taken, be it a family shelter, a friend or other family member's home; anyplace other than a tent encampment under a footbridge.

The scene that greeted the marshal and myself as we entered the lobby could have been choreographed by Macy's. The entire six-story building had turned out in celebration of the eviction. The residents stood two-deep along the corridor, wildly applauding. At least one of them was blowing a noisemaker. The city marshal, for his part, was uncomfortable in the brand-new role of grand marshal of his own parade of thanksgiving.

Normally, on his daily eviction rounds, a marshal is greeted with far less enthusiasm.

"My first-ever standing ovation," he quipped to me. "How do you like that?"

I thought it was all quite harmless and almost amusing in a dark sort of way, until someone in the crowd noticed me walking alongside the marshal, trying to remain as inconspicuous as possible.

Chapter 17. Both Sides Now

"Hey, who's that guy?" the man cried out, pointing at me.

"That's the f—king guy who's been trying to help [the defendants]," another resident screeched.

"Let's get the little bastard!" I heard someone else say. "String him up," another voice chimed in.

What up to that point had been a peaceful, cheering throng quickly devolved into a lynch mob, and I did not relish being the chief attraction.

As the crowd ominously closed ranks around us, the marshal stepped in front of me, raised his hands, and played the savior once again. My savior, this time.

"OK," he called out to the angry mob, "now everybody calm down. This guy here is just doing his job. There's a system we follow, and he's a part of it, same as me. But I know him, and I'm telling you he's a really decent guy. So, please, everyone go back to your apartments. It'll all be over soon."

And, hearing these words of peace emanate from their esteemed grand marshal, the mob melted away into the warmth of their own homes, and the eviction commenced as scheduled.

The family, while remaining adamant that they had done nothing to necessitate such a drastic measure, were fully cooperative with the marshal. However, they declined my offer of a taxicab ride. They had found a temporary home only a short distance away. It was a dank basement, offered to them by the building super, a friend of the client. Even with the large boiler in the center of the basement, there was room in there for a few beds and a small table.

I kept the case open after the eviction, as in my mind the grungy, unfinished basement was not an appropriate long-term housing option, especially for the two kids. The wife, who had lived for years under the most disagreeable of circumstances, made it known to me that all the grunge, coupled with the noxious odors of the basement, were too much, even for her unrefined tastes. I took her for a tour of a women's shelter in Brooklyn, to see if she might prefer staying there for a while, but she found it to be ... well, a homeless shelter, and she elected to stick it out with her family in the basement.

I did make a referral to ACS (Association of Children's Services) on behalf of the two kids, which garnered me a letter from the teenage son, threatening my life. But ACS hadn't been there to witness the horrors of the previous apartment and apparently did not view the family's present situation as necessitating a case for child abuse or neglect. That was their call, and I didn't quibble with it.

In any event, within weeks, the family managed to hook up with a non-profit social service agency that, miraculously, found them their own apartment in another part of town. As their worker, I was genuinely pleased for them, and hopeful that for the sake of everyone involved, they would mend their ways. Or, barring that, that their new neighbors would be possessed of very limited sensory powers.

Another case, years later, helped to further cement my growing belief that landlords—even corporations—can be as much victims as villains.

The true villain in this case was a woman of about 30, a highly-paid financial services professional who had reportedly injured her leg in an accident and was out on temporary disability. Later the story changed to her losing her job.

She lived in a rental studio in a luxury uptown Manhattan building. It was the kind of apartment that would make a roomy walk-in closet in a suburban McMansion, but in Manhattan cost $3500 a month. The client had exhausted her limited savings, or so she said, and could no longer afford that rent. She was a month in arrears when I got the case.

I could sense from the initial home visit that the client, who was playing the victim card for all it was worth, was not entirely on the up-and-up. Her list of physical complaints took up a full page of the initial assessment form. She had a fairly extensive (and expensive) wardrobe, with a loaded shoe tree as tall as an average Japanese maple.

She also played the feminine wiles card like a pro. But my misgivings aside, crisis managers don't get to choose their clients or their fights. So we psyched the client and got her a GAL, who quickly saw through her act, as did the doctors whose medical reports became part of the court record. Their diagnosis: "conversion disorder," which is a fancy way of saying the client's problems were psychosomatic in nature. Which, in itself, is a fancy way of saying she was faking the whole thing.

The case, as I remember, dragged on in Manhattan housing court for at least four months, through various motions and adjournments. The landlord's attorney—the only guy in the courtroom in a good suit—just kept shaking his head and smiling a wry smile. He'd seen this movie before, and he knew how it would end: with an eviction and a big, fat fee.

By the time the eviction finally took place, the client's rental arrears exceeded $18,000. Add the legal bills, and the landlord must have been out $30,000 or more.

I arrived for the eviction in advance of the marshal but was advised that the client had departed hours earlier. According to the doorman, she glided out of the lobby wheeling all her belongings to the curb, where she was picked up by a young man in a large van. She did not appear to have the same pronounced limp she had only days before.

"I think the driver was her boyfriend," said the doorman. "I had a feeling this lady knew exactly what she was doing and where she was going."

When the manager of the building showed up with the marshal, we all went up to see the apartment. Suffice it to say the client had not left it broom-clean.

"Good riddance," sighed the manager. "Sometimes there's nothing you can do with tenants like these, but go through the process and take your lumps."

I admit to feeling a little sorry for the travails of a large real estate holding company. And for the progressive son of a Communist mother, if that's not being non-judgmental, I'll be damned if I know what is.

Another client, this one out in Queens near JFK airport, seemed to get a kick out of pulling my chain. The landlord, who lived below him on the first floor, was evicting the client for gross misuse of the premises, among other things.

The client's apartment was littered with liquor bottles, and he hadn't paid his rent in some time, nor did he seem to want to. The client had no lease, and thus, no legal case. I pulled some strings, told some small lies, and managed, at considerable time and effort, to find the man a nice, clean room in one of the city's better adult homes. I even badgered my nephew into showing up with his truck to help transport the client's belongings to his new lodging.

On moving day, he emerged from his apartment with a bottle of scotch and a haughty grin.

"I don't want to live in no adult home," he said. "I've got another place you can take me."

It seems the client had a friend and she had agreed to take him in. At this point, I got testy.

"You know," I said to the guy, not trying to hide my annoyance, "you might have told me about your friend before I went through all the trouble of finding you a place to live."

"Sorry about that," he said, without much conviction, right before we dropped him off. "Why don't you come on up and we'll talk about it over a drink."

These types of client engagements caused me to approach the minefield of landlord-tenant relations with less credulity. It can be just as beneficial, I found, for a crisis manager to imagine walking in the shoes of a landlord as of a tenant. I know that if I had neighbors so thoroughly despicable that their eviction would inspire a building-wide celebration, I, too, would be out there on the parade ground, cheering on the marshal. But I most definitely would not have been the guy carrying the rope.

Over the years, immersion in APS helped me, in general, to be less judgmental toward others, like the adult children of my elderly clients.

There was, for example, a Bunyanesque widow living in a ramshackle house out in Far Rockaway, a stone's throw from the Atlantic Ocean. She had already rejected several attempts by a former APS worker to implement a heavy-duty cleaning and was now claiming that unnamed neighbors were peering through her bedroom window, making anonymous, threatening calls to her home in the nighttime and otherwise making her life a living hell.

But when I arrived, she didn't want to talk about the neighbors, only her seven rotten children, all of whom lived out of town with their own families, abandoning their poor mother to her own misery. She begged me to call her daughter in Virginia and use whatever influence I had to get her to come to New York and help out a mother in distress.

"She's the only child who will talk to me," the client said.

As requested, I phoned up the daughter. When she answered, I identified myself and explained why I was calling.

"Here's what you can do," said the daughter. "You can tell my mother to go f—k herself. Or, if you want, you can say it nicer. I really don't care how you phrase it."

And she hung up.

My first response was instinctual for a guy with a mother whose shortcomings didn't come close to meriting that kind of reaction. What kind of children would treat their lonely, widowed mother in such a way? No matter how petulant and splenetic she appeared to be, she was, after all, their one and only mother.

And then I spent some more time in that woebegone excuse for a home. The more we spoke, the more profanity (and racism) she spouted and the more hostility she showed toward the world at large, I began to wonder what kind of a mother she had been to her children during their formative years.

Bottom line: It would have been extremely presumptuous of me to judge either side harshly, without benefit of having been there from the beginning. Still, the fact that not a one of those seven adult children wanted anything to do with their mother spoke volumes.

That night, when I got home, I phoned up the folks down in Florida, and had a warm conversation with the old lady.

And I once more closed the case of the forsaken Far Rockaway mom, knowing full well that it would inevitably find its way back to our office and hoping that the next time it would land on someone else's desk.

And, finally, there are those clients that actually make you want to commiserate with your Uncle Sam. Those are the ones skimming and scamming along the fault lines of the social safety net.

Former President Ronald Reagan summed these people up with the all-purpose sobriquet, *welfare queen,* which to his right-wing base connoted that mythological African American figure living large on the government teat.

In all my years in the field, which includes APS and geriatric social services, I never once encountered such an individual. The scammers to whom I refer were all low-level offenders. Not sympathetic, by any means, but hardly the villainous gargoyles fantasized by the right.

One I remember vividly lived in the same SRO dwelling as my client, Tobias. He was a husky Caucasian man of about 30 who worked full-time, off-the-books, in his cousin's garage. He had somehow managed to get himself on Supplemental Security Income and food stamps, and he seemed quite proud of that accomplishment.

He had referred himself to APS because, like Tobias, he was about to be evicted from the rooming house. His housing case was defenseless, so there wasn't a whole lot I could do for him on that score. But I will confess that what I would have liked to do was report him to the appropriate authorities.

But APS workers are not supposed to let their emotions override their obligations to their clients.

Which includes not ratting them out to the feds.

CHAPTER 18

Thwarting the Gypsies

*From the fire her face was all aglow/How she enchanted
me/Oh, how I'd like to hold her near/And kiss and forever
whisper in her ear.*
— Brian Hyland, "Gypsy Woman"

When I was a freshman in college, I thought briefly about becoming a cop. I'd played a lot of cops-and-robbers in the backyard when I was a kid—does one ever stop being a kid?—and, at that time, what I wanted after graduation was a job that was challenging, eventful, and dangerous.

The dangerous part came from the guilt over being in college rather than Vietnam, which was where teenagers who didn't go to college in 1966 usually ended up. I remain comfortable with the decision to forego the war, which I believed to be immoral and pointless, then and now. But 54 years later, I'm still on that guilt trip and will likely be on it for the rest of my life.

However, as it turned out, the law enforcement career plan was moot. The New York City Police Department back then had a very rigid 5'10" minimum height requirement. Not a skinny millimeter less would suffice. I, on the other hand, stood but 5'8-1/4". So unless I was willing to get on the torture rack and coax another inch-and-three-quarters out of my Lilliputian frame, cops and robbers was not in my future.

Not that it matters all these years later, but it irks me, just a little, to see cops the size of Danny DeVito out there on the beat.

So, when the opportunity did finally arise at Adult Protective Services for an undersized case manager to play copper for an afternoon, naturally, I leaped at it.

The alleged crime was financial exploitation of the elderly, a very common one at New York City APS and in every part of this country. But the circumstances of this case were somewhat unusual.

The client, an elderly gentleman of declining mental acuity, had

116

fallen completely under the spell of a young Gypsy woman, part of a Romani clan that had long ago settled in Flushing, Queens, and was well known to the local constabulary.

Up to this point, I wasn't aware that such enchantments still befell 21st century American males, even demented ones. I didn't realize how deep remains the craving for a mythological creature who dances around a campfire with hair dark as night and the fiery eyes of a cat.

But this guy was all-in on a classic swindle that dates all the way back to Moses.

The Gypsy had convinced the client that he was everything she had ever dreamed of in a man, and that she would one day belong only to him. But, until that time, she was in need of financial assistance for herself and her struggling family.

The elementary scam worked like this:

The Gypsy would phone up the client—sometimes at his home, sometimes in the senior citizen center where he would regularly go for lunch—and instruct him to go to his bank located a few blocks from his apartment and withdraw a certain amount of money. The Gypsy would meet him in front of his apartment building, give him a quick hug and a peck on the cheek and make off with the day's haul. This had been going on for weeks, if not months.

The case had come into APS as a fairly straightforward request from his daughter for assistance in obtaining affordable home care, as the client was in need of help with his "instrumental activities of daily living"—specifically, cooking, housekeeping, and laundry.

The flimflam was brought to my attention by staff at the senior center, who had become aware of the old man's relationship with the Gypsy woman and his frequent withdrawals from the bank.

I don't recall offhand whether it was I or the center staff who reported this to the police. In any case, I hooked up with a bunco squad detective who'd been tracking the nefarious activities of this extended Gypsy family for years.

The client, who wasn't in denial of what was going on—his denial was related solely to the Gypsy's motives—had made it known at the center that he was expecting her call that afternoon. The center director contacted me and I rushed over there to wait for the call. The detective, meanwhile, arranged to meet me outside the center and, together, we would track the client to the bank and back to his home, where we would confront the perpetrator and, hopefully, scare her off the grift.

As scheduled, the Gypsy phoned, and the client put on his coat and

"He probably won't shoot you"

hat and headed out for their rendezvous. The cop and I stealthily tailed him to the bank—where he withdrew another $500 from his savings account—and across the street and down two more blocks to his apartment lobby.

The Gypsy was waiting there, with an infant in her arms, along with another Gypsy woman with two Gypsy toddlers in tow. The women looked to be in their mid- to late 30s and whatever they had that was enchanting this old man, I couldn't find it for the life of me. To my mind, both women looked tired and haggard, maybe from all that running around in the heat and the effort it takes to sustain a long-running street hustle.

When we showed up on the scene, the gypsies appeared startled, but maintained their cool. It takes more than a lone cop and a crisis manager to rattle a couple of old pros. The client, for his part, was more perturbed.

"So, what's going on here?" asked the cop, after identifying himself.

"Everything's fine, officer," the client croaked. "These are my friends, and I'm helping them out."

The cop took aside the women and the three kids—most likely, kids they'd borrowed for the effect—and spoke bluntly to them about elder abuse and what might happen to them if they continued to run this particular scam.

Everybody knew that without a victim's complaint, which would not be forthcoming, there was no criminal case to be made here. But the hope was that, armed with the knowledge that the police were on to them, the gypsies would at least consider backing off this mark. After all, they'd been fleecing the poor *gadjo* for quite some time and had probably already gone through a sizeable portion of his assets.

Working with the daughter, APS put in Medicaid home care, and the home attendant proved to be a dedicated patient advocate and super-diligent about protecting the old man from further prevarications from avaricious gypsies.

Just a quick side note:

While the lure of the Gypsy Queen has maintained its hold on the popular imagination for centuries, it may be no match for modern technology. Many of the tried-and-true rackets perfected by the Romani have been overshadowed by more efficient and sophisticated computer and telemarketing scams targeting that same vulnerable senior demographic.

I was recently informed that in the wake of the aforementioned

118

case, APS was called in again, this time in support of those very same gypsies, who were facing eviction.

The lesson here being that today's perpetrator may be tomorrow's client. Just another roll of the APS Mandala.

CHAPTER 19

Wretched Refuse

If you walk through a lobby door and the awful stench almost knocks you off your feet, dollars to donuts it's coming from your client's apartment.
—Eugene, an APS supervisor of astute perspicacity

I remember my mother barging into my bedroom when I was a kid pleasantly passing the time, shooting baskets over the door with a pair of rolled-up sweat socks. She would look around the room at the dirty clothes, the unmade bed and the comic books and baseball cards strewn all about.

Her response was almost always the same.

"One of these days," she would admonish me, "you're going to wind up a Collyer brother."

I looked up the Collyer Brothers at our local library and read all about them in old, microfilmed newspaper clippings. It's a good thing that microfilm doesn't pack the emotional wallop of a movie or TV show, at least for a 13-year-old, as I would have been sleepless for weeks.

For those unfamiliar with dysfunctional American history, Homer and Langley Collyer were brothers who lived during the first half of the last century in a brownstone at the corner of 128th Street and Fifth Avenue. For years after the death of their mother, they lived relatively normally in their inherited building. They socialized with friends and continued working, Homer as an attorney and Langley a piano dealer. They even taught Sunday school together.

But, as fate would have it, Homer became blind and was forced to give up his legal practice, and his brother quit his job to care for him at home. And then, gradually, driven in large part by a racist fear that their Harlem neighborhood was being overtaken by hostile African American forces, they went into total seclusion while developing a joint obsession with collecting things; most notably furniture, books, newspapers and musical instruments. Their once-habitable dwelling turned into a huge

120

maze of walls and tunnels, with an estimated 140 *tons* of junk piled floor to ceiling and the brothers huddled down in tiny "nests" within those giant piles.

Just for comparison's sake, 140 tons of junk is about 40 percent heavier than a Boeing 757 and the same weight as the average Blue Whale, the largest animal to have ever walked the earth or swam its seas.

The Collyers' eccentric habits became widely known throughout the neighborhood, and their brownstone drew crowds of curious onlookers. Teenagers would throw rocks at the windows, which the brothers boarded-up. An unfounded rumor that the Collyers had large sums of cash and other valuables stashed away under the rubbish spurred a number of attempts at breaking and entering, thwarted by booby traps laid by Langley, who had a real flair for mechanical engineering.

In 1947, the brothers finally fell victims to their mutual hoarding disorder. On a tip from a source, police, after squeezing through the door and wading through the garbage, found Homer in his bathrobe, his matted hair down to his shoulders, dead of starvation and heart disease. Authorities discovered his brother a few weeks later, only feet from where Homer had expired. Langley's decomposing body, partially eaten by rats, was covered by stacks of newspapers, a suitcase and some metal bread boxes. He had apparently tripped one of the booby trap wires while trying to reach his paralyzed brother through a tunnel, and had been crushed to death.

So this is what my mother envisioned as the future of her only son. I didn't take her warnings too seriously, as the old lady was prone to hyperbolic outbursts (really, Mom, a pair of sweaty socks and a few dozen baseball cards, and you've got me pegged as rat food!).

The tale of Homer and Langley, to my pre-teen mind, was less a life lesson than a specter that adults impart to kids to scare the hell out of them, like the Baba Yaga or the dentist.

I never imagined that one day Homer and Langley would enter my life in a visceral way on an almost weekly basis, as I witnessed the privations and degradation wrought by the spiritual descendants of the legendary brothers.

At APS, cases of extreme hoarding were known as "Collyer cases."

Hoarding 101

The clinical literature—and it is as plentiful as it is dry—defines a compulsive hoarding situation as living spaces so cluttered that they cannot be used for their intended purposes; causing significant distress or impairment in normal life functioning; often affecting others living in that environment; and featuring an inability on the hoarder's part to discard items that appear to others as worthless.

Animal hoarding is, shall we say, a different animal. There is little in the way of empirical study on this subject, but its definition is based not on the number of animals being housed but the level of care provided to those animals (the 98 cats who once shared a studio apartment with one of my clients would most likely have quibbled with that definition—more on them later).

Most important: hoarding is a behavior, not a diagnosis, and may or may not be related to a severe, persistent mental illness. The jury is still officially out on the precise roles that schizophrenia, obsessive-compulsive disorder, or anorexia nervosa may play in hoarding behavior. This behavior, however, has been found in about 20 to 40 percent of OCD patients, suggesting a strong link.

The literature further points to hoarders as being prone to having attention deficit disorder, problems in forming emotional attachments, avoiding tasks (paying bills, washing dishes, etc.), and holding erroneous beliefs about their possessions (i.e., believing that every item has a special significance or will be needed down the road).

This concludes our introduction to hoarding.

And now, down to cases.

My first hoarding client was assigned only a few weeks into the job. She was no Collyer, but she gave a reasonable impression of one.

A middle-aged schoolteacher, thin and wiry of build, and displaying a considerable array of nervous tics, she had stocked her one-bedroom apartment with many years' worth of classroom remnants: student notebooks, drawings, collages, and mobiles. She complemented her students' output with countless unopened boxes of mail-order clothing, never-used (and expensive) camera equipment, at least several hundred dollars in small bills and enough quarters to keep every parking meter in Brooklyn ticking for months.

The expansive mess covered every available inch of floor space and rose to as high as three or four feet in some spots. The only positive was the lack of aromatic garbage, a staple of so many hoarding situations.

The four-man heavy-duty cleaning crew, who all hailed from Mexico or Central America, taught me a word I hadn't learned in four years of high school and college Spanish:

Chapter 19. Wretched Refuse

"Basura," a word that in its brevity somehow captures every conceivable form of human-generated trash.

I thought it odd that I'd read fully half of Don Quixote in the original Spanish and Cervantes had never once mentioned basura. He had, however, addressed the subject of windmills, and the futility of tilting at them, and this, rather than garbage, was my go-to metaphor for my years at APS.

The crew embarked on what would become a Stygian four-day cleaning exercise, leaving just me and the client watching them work from outside the door. Me, with a look of stunned disbelief; the client with a look of sheer terror.

She sweated, fidgeted, sobbed, and contorted her body throughout that first distressful day, as the cleaning guys skimmed a few tons of garbage off the top of the pile and into 50-pound plastic bags. I don't know what the current protocol is for HDC's, but back then, workers went out alone, without benefit of a psychiatrist or any mental health professional to assist clients on the verge of decompensating.

I have no idea how the two of us made it through that first, endless day. I remember holding her hand a lot and telling her that she was strong enough to get through it. I doubt she heard a word I said.

At various times, the client and I plodded into the belly of the beast to retrieve items of real value. I must have recovered a dozen Nikon cameras, more than 30 packages from Land's End, and a couple of hundred bucks from the middle of the pile.

The client, for her part, did not seem to care at all about the value of the individual items. It was for her, I think, the total experience of losing everything that had given her comfort, companionship and protection. In other words, all the things that for so long had taken the place of human relationships (although the client did acknowledge having a boyfriend, himself a major hoarder, who lived somewhere out on Staten Island).

Day One completely exhausted both of us. As the workers dragged the day's multi-ton haul into the elevator and down to the removal trucks, the client crept back into her apartment for a few moments of peaceful solitude and contemplation. There was a lone cleaning guy still in the apartment, a nondescript fellow about 5'5" with an innocent-looking, semi-permanent grin. After the client had re-entered the premises, he approached the door and locked it from the inside.

Talk about a bad vibe.

I banged, forcefully, on the door.

"Hey, open up! What's going on in there?"

I kept banging until the client came out a few minutes later. She appeared to be fine, but a little disheveled. The cleaning guy slipped past me without a word.

"Are you okay?" I inquired. "Did anything happen in there."

"No," she said. "Nothing happened at all."

I didn't believe her for a second.

On Day Two, before the crew arrived, I asked again about the incident. And she told me what had transpired between herself and the young man.

As she laid upon a thick carpet of yellowed scratch paper and unused sweaters, closing her eyes to ease her tortured psyche, the cleaning guy had crawled up alongside and mounted her.

"No, please," she said to him, gently but firmly. "I can't do this right now."

With a forlorn look, the cleaning guy wordlessly slid off her.

"And that's the whole story?" I asked.

"That's all there was," she said. "It was really no big deal. In fact, he seemed kind of sweet in a way. It just wasn't what I wanted."

For the rest of Day Two, I kept a very close eye on the guy, who must have known that I knew, as he maintained a low profile throughout the HDC. The second day, on balance, went better than the first. The client seemed more relaxed and didn't gasp every time a heaping shovelful of paper got poured into a Hefty bag. Indeed, you could actually begin to see slivers of scuffed wood floor peeking out of the debris.

I reported the failed attempt at sexual congress to my supervisor, who reported it to her superior, and there arose a hue and cry at the highest levels of the organization. I was asked by one higher-up how I allowed the client to be alone with a would-be predator. I must say that I didn't much care for his tone.

On Day Three, the offending worker did not show up at all. Nor would he ever show up again, having been summarily fired by the trash removal company.

The client, for her part, took the news of his dismissal hard. It appeared, at least to me, that she had transferred some of her apprehensions about losing her stuff to the tribulations of the cleaning guy.

"He didn't do anything wrong," the client kept insisting. "All he wanted, really, was a little tenderness. It makes me sad that I didn't have it to give."

Day Three went off about the same as Day Two. Nobody tried to have weird sex with anyone else, and at day's conclusion, you could see the outlines emerging of what had been, once upon a time, a perfectly livable dwelling.

The final day was by far the easiest. The client, by this point, had settled into a mellower groove. She laughed at a few bad jokes and even told one or two. She also took some comfort in the fact that her landlord would no longer be threatening eviction.

What happened after those four days is something of a blur. I had a psych evaluation done with the goal of getting the client into treatment that might help keep her from resurrecting the clutter. Recidivism among hoarders is extremely common.

"Generally, unless the heavy duty cleaning is followed by a lot of very good drug and talk therapy," a clinical psychologist once advised me, "you'll be back in there in three to six months, dealing with the same amount of crap."

In a worst case, I figured it would take this client considerably longer than that to get to her previous level. She had lost her teaching job and no longer had access to hundreds of pieces of student paperwork every day.

Some months later, the client reportedly fell into rental arrears that totaled in the thousands of dollars and elected to walk away from the apartment and move in with the boyfriend on Staten Island.

Over the years, teachers comprised an inordinately large percentage of my hoarding clients. I haven't seen anything in the clinical literature that would point to such a connection. Compulsive hoarders tend to be perfectionists who fear making mistakes; are subject to forgetting important things and missing deadlines and appointments; and have very poor insight into their own behaviors.

None of these, and other aforementioned characteristics, are more typical of educators than of any other profession.

Perhaps my most difficult hoarding case, at least from a logistical perspective, featured an elderly woman who lived in a 3rd floor walk-up apartment on 8th Avenue in the heart of midtown Manhattan. She was facing a nuisance holdover eviction due to the appalling condition of the home.

Still, the actual hoard was not particularly horrendous—it was a mere five or six-hour job, encompassing no more than 70 or 75 garbage bags (or roughly two tons' worth). The problem was that the cleaning people showed up late, and by the time they got to schlepping those two tons of fun down two narrow flights of stairs and dumping it over the already grubby Manhattan street corner, it was the height of the evening rush hour.

For all you lucky readers who live in places that don't have rush hours, picture this scene as it might have been imagined by Hieronymus Bosch, Albrecht Dürer, or any master of the apocalyptic arts:

Tens of thousands of commuters emerging from their offices, heading toward the subways or the Port Authority Bus Terminal at 42nd Street. Thousands of passenger cars, and taxicabs driven by maniacs, heading north in the direction of the 59th Street bridge, with horns blaring and angry motorists inventing fresh forms of invective on the fly. Add to this everyday mayhem hundreds more people attempting to queue up at the bus stop, which happened to be located right outside the client's building and was now rapidly disappearing under five-foot piles of rubbish.

And that's just what was happening on the outside. Taking place inside the building was another level of chaos. The hyperventilating landlord was hollering at the cleaning guys for inadvertently spilling the contents of a trash bag on the stairwell, and the neighbors were in an uproar over having their dinners interrupted by the scent of a rich bouquet of refuse.

I would have liked to be upstairs attending to my client's fluid mix of anxiety and depression, but instead I had to be out there on 8th Avenue, negotiating with the traffic manager from the Metropolitan Transit Authority. He was justifiably concerned about having his passengers scrambling over a landfill just for the pleasure of scrunching into an overcrowded bus.

The traffic manager had no doubt navigated his way through enough rush-hour debacles to have written a book of his own, and this created a sort of bond between us, the kind that can only be forged by a mutual understanding of the insanity that lies just below the surface of daily life in the Naked City.

"Have you ever heard of Adult Protective Services?" I asked him.

"No," he replied. "What's that?"

"It's what you're standing in right now," I said.

Anyway, the dump truck finally arrived, and it didn't take long for the workmen to load it up. Once the rubbish was on its merry way, my pulse, and the pulse of a city always on the move, returned to normal. And my client got a much-needed reprieve from the city marshal.

All told, not a bad outcome.

A former colleague had the considerable misfortune of catching a massive hoarding case on her very first day on the job.

Chapter 19. Wretched Refuse

The client, a single Orthodox Jewish male who lived with his sister, was referred by a visiting nurse who was concerned that his diabetes was out of control, and he was being resistant to out-patient treatment.

The client greeted his newbie APS worker at the door ("He was a little annoyed that I was Black.") before excusing himself to get a shovel. The worker's immediate reaction, having had no prior knowledge of hoarding disorders, was that the man intended to use it upside her head.

"I was praying to myself, please God, don't let this crazy racist kill me," she says.

When he returned with the implement, he explained, "I've got to clear a path for you to get in."

The worker was relieved, but confused.

Once inside the premises, her confusion turned to shock, as the home's impeccably maintained exterior did not hint at the unholy mess therein.

"I'd never seen anything like this in 30 years of child welfare work," she notes. "Mounds and mounds of old computer parts, picked up on the street, but also knitting machines and balls of yarn collected by the sister, and, most horrifying of all, kosher bags full of spoiled food covered in fleas.... I got those flea bites all over my legs."

The Orthodox Jew again expressed reluctance about dealing with a Black woman, so the case manager wisely phoned up her immediate supervisor and asked him to slap on his yarmulke and get right over. His presence on the scene succeeded in calming the restive client.

"Herman was a terrific supervisor," she says. "First thing he says to me when he gets to the house, 'Welcome to APS!'"

On the day of the HDC, it was not the client, but his sister, who flipped her wig.

"When the crew goes into the apartment, she dashes into the street, screaming that a n---ga is taking over her house, and two of her neighbors come running down the block to see what's going on," recalls the case manager. "And when they walk inside, their mouths just open with amazement and disbelief. The sister thought she'd get support from her community, but not after the community got a good look at what was going on inside."

The upshot:

The HDC was completed, but the client's failure to get his diabetes under control wound up costing him his leg. The worker kept the case open for a full year, until he was placed in a nursing home. As for his sister, her status within her community had been irretrievably lost.

"He probably won't shoot you"

Like clients and Tolstoy's families, no two hoards are quite alike.

There are, for example, specialty hoarders, who focus on a single garbage genre.

Like the musician living in a pre-war, upper Manhattan building, who hoarded pianos, cellos, drum kits, and brass instruments. He was a charming fellow, with a fairly impressive list of musical credits and collaborators. But he was perpetually short on cash, and late with the rent.

I pointed out the possibility of selling some of the gear to raise the rent money, which I knew to be a non-starter. A clarinet player by trade, the euphoniums and tubas in the apartment were of no use to him. But, of course, use is the last thing that matters to a hoarder, even a specialty one.

Ultimately, I was able to obtain a grant from a charitable organization, which resolved the client's rent problem. I wished him well and invited him to check back with APS should he run out of breathing space in the apartment. I also mentioned that I was thinking of taking up the accordion, and if he were ever to locate one under his immense musical pile, I'd be interested in taking it off his hands for a reasonable fee.

Another specialty hoarder out in Queens favored bicycles: girls and boys, all speeds. In the midst of the heavy-duty cleaning, I remember him stepping out for a brief walk to clear his head. He came back with a busted Schwinn draped over his shoulder.

"I have to be honest with you," I reproached him. "This doesn't look like you're serious about relieving this situation."

"I know," he said, sheepishly. "I need to work on it."

This was one of those hoarding cases that would almost definitely be back in our office in three to six months.

Other such hoarders included the handyman referenced back in Chapter 3 whose genre was discarded auto parts and the elderly Korean-American with thousands of history books stacked neatly on library shelves. The problem wasn't the books; it was the shelves that were closing in on the client like prison walls.

Yet another specialist hoarder client was a well-known figure in Brooklyn Democratic Party circles who displayed an unhealthy attachment to disabled computer parts—cracked monitors, disassembled printers, grease-encrusted keyboards. I'm sure there was an unconscious connection to be made between all those busted parts and the client's internal feelings of brokenness, but there was no time for all that. What we needed to accomplish in that moment was to beat the marshal to the punch and get all the stuff out of the apartment as soon as possible.

Rather than have a cleaning crew cart it all away for free, this client chose to pay handsomely for the services of a half-dozen moving men, three large box trucks, and a like number of large storage units. A bill that likely totaled $2,000 or more in moving costs, and thousands more in long-term storage expenses.

As I watched this sad man stuff the final item into the last truck—an old desk chair with wheels missing and all the upholstery peeled off—I couldn't help but ask the $64,000 question.

"Why would you want to save an old, broken-down chair?" I inquired.

"It's a perfectly fine chair," he countered. "In fact, I'm giving it as a birthday gift to my nephew."

And, with that, like a wagon master in Death Valley days, he hopped into the cab of the lead truck, and waved on the caravan as it departed with a full cargo.

As part of my immersion in *Basura* World, I also discovered that it is possible to be a hoarder of dirt; like a client in Queens who had not had his apartment cleaned or disinfected in many years. After resisting the HDC for months, and now faced with a holdover eviction and completely out of options, he finally relented.

The cleaning guys rolled in just like any other job, tossing out every rug, pulling up all the mucky and frayed carpeting, and throwing away hundreds of soup and vegetable cans so old that the expiration dates had worn off. They then washed down all the flooring, disinfected every counter surface and cabinet, and deodorized the whole apartment.

And when their job was done, I figured so was the holdover eviction case.

Not so fast.

The landlord, a smug son of a bitch, came in at the close of day to inspect the premises. I knew he detested my client and wanted him out of the building. I could somewhat relate to that, as the client was, himself, a cantankerous piece of work, and his neighbors were not shy about attesting to his lack of likability.

The landlord's initial reaction to the HDC was disturbing.

"This apartment is still filthy," the landlord sniggered. "I'm not satisfied."

"Hey, look," I responded. "The tenant has complied with all your demands. What more do you want the poor guy to do?"

"He probably won't shoot you"

The landlord walked arrogantly around the apartment, shaking his head and snickering while picking up tiny bits of carpet lint off the floor and running his hands over a couple of dusty shelves.

"Oh, okay," he said, grudgingly. "We'll let it go for now, as long as he promises to keep the place in good condition."

And, finally, there were the animal hoarders, who presented a whole different set of problems, as the refuse in these cases were sentient beings, often cute sentient beings.

That mother and daughter in Brooklyn who at one time shared their large studio apartment with the 98 cats (and, yes, you read that number correctly) were a memorable example.

By the time their case came to me, a lengthy, concerted effort on the part of the clients and animal control officers had reduced the feline population in the apartment to just two. An HDC was already in the books.

"How did you ever come to live with 98 cats?" I inquired of the daughter, who, if you casually encountered her on the street or in a shop, would not strike you as the Bartholomew Cubbins of pussycats.

"One cat at a time," was her answer.

But even with just two cats remaining in the flesh, the spirits of the other 96 still haunted the apartment, in the recrystallization of uric acid, especially irksome on humid summer days, and the permanent stains on the hardwood floor. The final HDC addressed these lingering issues with enzymatic cleaners, the only permanent solution to a severe cat odor problem.

"The cat count will never again get above two," the daughter promised.

I don't know why, but I believed her.

Cats and dogs, and, less often, rabbits and birds, are the varieties of household pets normally encountered on a hoard. I'm a dog person, myself, but I've lived with as many as four cats at one time, and a parrot that, despite years of prodding, refused to say "pieces of eight."

I was generally okay with all these harmless species. It was the rodent hoarders who tested my mettle.

I recall an elderly and frail Chinese American who occupied a dingy little studio in a lower Manhattan housing project. He was past being able to care for himself, and he was mostly oblivious to his surroundings, notably the bathroom faucet that ran 24-7. But he did somehow manage to keep all his rat roommates happy and well-fed.

I was more than a little put off when they emerged from their hiding places to have a bit of fun with the APS worker. During my initial visit, I remember the little rascals darting across the floor at supersonic speed, at one point scampering over my feet, which I should have had the good sense to elevate.

The old guy had money, so, naturally, there was a younger woman looking to assume control of his financial affairs. We psyched the client and applied for guardianship, and, in the meantime, commenced a heavy-duty cleaning and major rodent extermination.

It was the first time I'd ever seen a cleaning crew truly unnerved. It occurred when one of the men reached into a kitchen cabinet to place the poisoned beef and got a bite on the hand from a potential victim. The man's thick gloves kept him from requiring stiches and a tetanus shot.

To be quite honest, the bigger concern on my end was that the client might get hungry enough to eat the poisoned meat.

I was extremely happy when the guardianship came through and I could hand the client off to someone who had the legal authority to place him in a safe place. I made my last home visit with the Article 81 guardian in tow. I guess the rats didn't find the new guy to be as much fun, as they didn't come out to play that day.

At APS, you learn to be thankful for these tiny favors.

CHAPTER 20

Sons and Mothers

A man loves his sweetheart the most, his wife the best, but his mother the longest.
—Irish Proverb

I was talking to an old colleague who was recounting some APS war stories. She told a tale of a middle-aged client, a tall, gangly fellow who lived with his aging mother in a rental apartment not far from our old office. His mother was his sole purpose in life, and apart from her, there were no family members, friends, or acquaintances. It was just the two of them rattling around in a drafty fourth-floor walkup.

In psychological terms, they lived in what's known as a homeostatic balance, where all the mother's and son's needs and desires were met by each other. It may not have been an especially cheerful way to live for either of them, but it was a stable one.

Until it wasn't.

Just like a bacteria or virus disrupts the natural homeostasis of the human body, a homeostatic relationship can undergo disturbances that create a "negative state of tension" in one or both parties.

In this case, the disruption came in the form of the illness and death of the mother, vastly complicated by the son's diagnosed severe, persistent mental illness, and his non-compliance with his medications and talk therapy.

The client himself reportedly had no income of his own. His mother had been paying the rent and all other expenses. So when she and her Social Security were gone, the rental arrears began to mount until the landlord sought eviction in housing court. The death of his mother, combined with the threat of homelessness and having no one else in his life to whom to turn for support, pushed the client's already fragile mental state to the brink.

On that fateful eviction day, the city marshal and the case manager went to the apartment and were met by the client, who had an eviction plan of his own. He opened the door to the marshal, scurried to the nearest window and leaped several floors to his death.

Call it the final disruption.

Suddenly, I felt my body tingle. This story sounded so very familiar. "Oh, my God," I said. "I remember this story! This was once my case!"

Indeed, I did have a tall, gangly client in his late 40s or 50s—call him Harry—who lived in that same neighborhood with *his* aging, dying mother. But the more details I recalled from my long-ago case, the clearer it became that these were separate cases. Like what we used to say back in elementary school: it's the same thing, but different.

My guy lived on a high floor of a large cooperative apartment building. And he had money of his own—enough to pay expenses when his mother was gone.

This client had been distrustful of me, occasionally to the point of exhibiting a mildly threatening hostility, grounded in severe paranoia. For weeks, I'd been bringing him to his psychotherapy appointments at a local mental health clinic. His therapist kept closing his case due to poor attendance and a recalcitrant attitude, and I kept persuading her to re-open it. But, finally, the client had exhausted her patience, and his talk therapy was terminated for good.

I remembered the mother, softly turning and groaning in her bed in the living room, her ankles swollen and discolored, deep grooves etched into her face. She was not much for communicating by that point, and even without any intimate knowledge of her medical history, I reckoned that she would not be with us much longer.

I worried at that time about what might befall the man once his life purpose was gone.

But before things came to a head, I moved to another APS contracting agency and the case was transferred to my replacement.

I have no idea what happened to the guy. I would like to think that in his mother's absence, he would have discovered a pathway healthier than a plunge out the window, perhaps a new roommate and a new life purpose. But I knew enough not to be at all sanguine about his prospects.

Sons and mothers, mothers and sons.

These were some of my most disheartening cases: the over-mothered, *smothered* men, and what happens to them when they become motherless. These cases seemed to range from the deeply sad, to the creepy-sad, to the incredibly creepy-sad.

I remember one client in his 50s or 60s who had murdered his mother in what was without doubt a mercy killing. He had lived with her all his life, and her debilitating illness came with chronic, unspeakable pain, unbearable to both of them. This wasn't my case but given that APS was walking in on an active crime scene, the boss wanted the assigned worker to have back-up support.

The poor man sat silently at his kitchen table, in an almost fugue-like state, surrounded by cops, APS workers, and a therapist, who tried to engage the client in conversation. His mother's body, to my recollection, was in the bedroom, awaiting the coroner. It was one of the dreariest scenes I'd ever encountered.

"I understand, she was your purpose," the therapist kept saying to the man, hoping to elicit a reaction. Finally, when she took his hand in hers, the man responded, in a cascade of tears. I looked at the cops. They were a little teary-eyed themselves. I assumed the very last thing they wanted to do in that moment was read the man his Miranda rights and slap on the handcuffs. But that's ultimately what they did.

A former supervisor had a strikingly similar case during his tenure as a worker, this one with a slightly different ending. Not murder this time, just natural causes. The worker, on his last home visit, had attempted to convince the son of a widowed client to allow home care to be put in place for her. But the son vehemently refused, so intent was he in not having another person usurp his life's purpose.

Before the next monthly home visit, a call from a neighbor reported an unpleasantly pungent odor emanating from the home, one unmistakable to soldiers in combat and morgue attendants. The worker went back to find the son sitting in the living room, his mother propped up beside him on the couch. She had been dead since the day after the worker's last visit.

The son was nearly catatonic. The worker tried to speak with him, but no response was forthcoming. They waited wordlessly, the two of them, for the authorities to arrive.

"This case really shook Jack," says a former colleague of the caseworker. "He was the only person who had been permitted to enter their closed world. It took him a while to get over it."

Another colleague had a case that was even harder to let go.

A severely developmentally disabled son who was, at the time of the APS worker's initial visit, at a neighborhood drug store buying condoms.

The client, his 80-year-old mother, noted that, for her son's

134

purposes, there was really no need for contraception, as she was the object of his desire.

"Better he does it to me," she told her incredulous case manager, "than he go out into the street and rape some other woman."

The worker explained to the client that those were not the only two alternatives, and offered to get some help for both she and her son.

"No," the mother was adamant. "I would just rather he do me."

There is no law against an adult male having consensual sex with his biological mother, if she is of sound mind and body. But, in this case, the outcome was the placement of the client in a skilled nursing facility, where the romantic overtures, if any, would come from folks her own age.

Still another case of mother and son locked in interminable homeo-stasis puts the lie to the notion that money can buy happiness. In this case, the mother was my client, and her live-in son, a postal worker, had likewise devoted all his adult life to her care and feeding, at the expense of any other companionship or any life that belonged to him alone.

The two lived in a modest rental apartment—only somewhat more elaborately-furnished than Ralph and Alice Kramden's. I was ready to apply for Medicaid home care for the client, who needed more help around the apartment than her son could provide. But the drab sur-roundings masked the fact that the couple had somehow managed over these many years to squirrel away millions of dollars in stocks and bonds. I couldn't fathom how these two had amassed that much wealth, unless the client's son had been using the mail as his personal ATM. In any case, I tossed the Medicaid application.

What the client really needed most at this point was a reputable estate planner. I brought one into her home, but before the client had the opportunity to sign any documents, she passed away suddenly, leav-ing the son as sole beneficiary of the entire fortune. He was not pre-pared, intellectually or emotionally, to handle an inheritance of that size. He was resistant—passively resistant—to all suggestions that he consider drawing up a will or a trust, to ensure that upon his death, his wishes on the disbursement of his assets would be honored. It is unlikely he would have taken any such empowering steps, even if he hadn't got-ten cancer and joined his mother in the afterlife within a year.

The kind of money we're talking about rarely stays unclaimed for long. And, indeed, it wasn't very long before a deputation of cousins, nieces, and nephews—none of whom had any significant contact with mother or son while they were living—made themselves known to the

Public Administrator's office. And they walked away with the whole kit and caboodle, minus the attorney fees, the court fees, and the genealogist's bill.

"This may sound a bit cruel," the lawyer told me at the time, "but all those relatives, whoever they are, will get a lot more joy out of that money than mother and son ever would."

Cruel, perhaps. But, sadly, also quite true.

CHAPTER 21

Smoothing Over
the Humiliation

One of the aspects of the job that I found most distasteful was the kind of pointless and thoughtless referral that only brings pain and humiliation to a client and his or her family.

Such referrals come in two distinct forms: the aforementioned cover your ass referrals that are made strictly to take another social service organization off the hook, and unfounded referrals aimed at embarrassing a perceived enemy. These I call "weaponized referrals."

In the early 1900s, the upper Manhattan neighborhood called Harlem witnessed the "Great Migration," as tens of thousands of ambitious African Americans fled the depredations of the post–Reconstruction South in search of a less oppressive living environment in which to raise their families, and better job opportunities. This migration reached its zenith in the wake of the First World War, which created massive numbers of new industrial jobs in the northern states.

The Great Migration, which lasted roughly from 1910 into the early 1930s, spawned the Harlem Renaissance, an explosion of creativity and intellectualism encompassing the worlds of literature, poetry, music, and theater. Major contributors to this age of enlightenment, also known as the "New Negro Movement," included Paul Robeson, Louis Armstrong, Josephine Baker, Langston Hughes, and the poet Countee Cullen.

The glory of the Harlem Renaissance lives on in the work of all the great African American artists who came later, musicians and writers to whom it remains an inspirational touchstone. Its glory is further reflected in the magnificent, multi-storied homes that surround the West Harlem campus of the City University of New York. A section of this area known as Striver's Row features the very finest of these architectural marvels—a collection of townhouses built in the Georgian Revival, Colonial Revival and Italian Renaissance Revival styles.

These are the homes that are still to this day inhabited by the descendants of the hard-working Black folks who made it big in New York, seizing all the opportunities created by The Great Migration to grab that elusive American Dream by the throat.

In one sense, it felt like an honor to enter one of those stately homes for the first time and experience a little of the aura of that storied period in American history. It was also one of the most disconcerting and discouraging visits in all my APS years.

The client and family patriarch was a retired civil attorney of legendary legal stature who was suffering from late-stage Alzheimer's dementia. Nevertheless, he still retained his dignity in both his posture and manner—tall and erect, gentle and courtly, with an air of self-deprecating humor. He wore a gray suit and tie around the house and showed me his humidor full of expensive cigars. (My grandfather, a dignified and courtly gentleman in his own right, was the only other man I ever knew who owned a humidor.)

The client's wife was a retired oncologist, his son a chief of cardiac surgery at a major hospital, and his daughter a writer and university professor. The grandkids were all professionals of one kind or another or training to become professionals. If one were to visit this home 50 years from now, one would likely be greeted by the president of the World Bank or the Nobel prizewinner in physics. Everything in that house, from the high ceilings to the parquet floors to the well-stocked library, bespoke *accomplishment* and *striving*.

This CYA referral had come from a hospital social worker who reported being very concerned about the client's safety in the home. Prior to his recent hospitalization, the client had wandered away from the house during the night in his pajamas, lost and disoriented, ultimately winding up in the middle of the West Side Highway, and causing a hell of a traffic snarl. That he survived that night was testament to a life well-lived and of very good fortune.

During his brief stay in the hospital, the family installed locks on both front and rear doors and hired a home health aide to be with the client 24 hours a day, seven days a week when he returned home. In short, the problem had already been resolved, and with a simple phone call, the hospital social worker could have easily ascertained that fact and saved the family the humiliation of an APS visit.

Chapter 21. Smoothing Over the Humiliation

Writing in *Psychology Today*, Dr. Neel Burton describes the act of humiliation as having one's "status claims" undermined, with an accompanying abasement of dignity and the loss of standing in one's community.

Indeed, notes Burton, humiliation calls into question the authority to make those status claims in the first place, "leaving people stunned and speechless, and more than that, voiceless."

It further stands to reason that the more elevated the status claim, the more precipitous the loss of dignity, especially when the family in question is African American and humiliation deliveryman is white.

And not just any white man, but a lawful representative of the sovereign State of New York. Burton argues that what impedes a rapid recovery from such a humiliating episode is its public nature. When New York State is, in effect, pronouncing you unable to care for your family, I'd call that pretty public.

So, there I was on a late spring afternoon, standing uncomfortably in the family living room, like an uninvited and unwelcome dinner guest. Still, I had a job to do there. I asked the appropriate questions and confirmed that the appropriate measures to ensure the client's safety had been put in place.

But, most important, I took pains during my visit to validate the feelings of a family which had been emotionally violated. In particular, I focused on the wife, who was close to tears throughout the length of the visit, clearly overwhelmed by the indignity of it all.

There was nothing I could do about my pale complexion. So I did whatever I could, in words and body language, to let this woman know that I knew that this referral was a big mistake that would be immediately rectified.

"I understand that this is painful for you," I told her. "And I am deeply sorry to have put you through it. I appreciate how cooperative you and your family have been."

I'm pretty sure that these feelings of humiliation didn't linger too long, probably barely longer than my own discomfort. After all, I had gotten into this business to help people who needed my help; not make people who didn't need my help feel like dirt.

Yet, the visit was not a complete loss on my end. I'd gotten a small taste of a grand American Renaissance. And Heaven only knows whether I'll be around to witness another.

The signs, so far, are not encouraging.

"He probably won't shoot you"

Weaponized referrals tend to occur less frequently than do CYA's, but even one is too many.

I had a case in Manhattan where a neighbor living a few doors down from the client reported seeing her private-pay aide browbeating the client on numerous occasions in the building lobby and hallway. The referral also referenced the poor condition of the client's apartment and hinted at the possibility of serious elder abuse and neglect.

I knew the referral was hinky the moment I walked into the home, which was spotlessly clean and beautifully furnished, with a refrigerator full of fresh, healthy foods and a bathroom floor off of which you could eat them. The client and her aide seemed to be more old friends than employer and employee. They related to each other the way old friends do—sharing their histories, opinions, and harmless fallibilities.

The client appeared to have a mild cognitive impairment, enough to largely diminish the embarrassment of an unwanted visit from a nosy APS worker. The aide was more upset about it. I didn't provide the name of the referral source, but the aide knew her identity without being told.

It seems the RS, the co-op's designated gossipmonger, did not think that the aide had shown her sufficient deference on one afternoon in the courtyard. She also resented that the client, who had once been her best friend, had found a new best friend in her home attendant.

"She's a very nasty lady," said the aide. "I'll never know what makes people so nasty."

After getting all the necessary information, I stuck around a little longer making small talk with these good folks, and apologizing for the inconvenience, which I assured them would not be repeated.

"That's all right," said the client. "We like it whenever a nice young man like you stops by to chat."

CHAPTER 22

Who's That Hogging My Bathroom?

Humor requires no other justification or defense than laughter.
—Neil Shaeffer, *The Art of Laughter*

When it came to laughing in the face of the quotidian disasters at APS, my thoughts would often turn to the brilliant, choleric comedy of Lenny Bruce. In one of my very favorite Bruce routines, a flight attendant rushes into the cockpit to advise the captain that the rear of the aircraft has just been blown apart and the passengers are being sucked out into the abyss.

To which the pilot replies, "Boy, are we gonna get yelled at!"

As discussed in other chapters, laughter at APS often treads perilously along the thinnest of lines between what psychologists call "the ludicrous context," and what is the cold, hard reality. I walked that line just about every day, with one lone exception:

Dementia.

Forgive me, comedy gods, but I didn't see the laughs. Even Lenny Bruce, who was absolutely fearless when it came to dissecting the most taboo subjects, to the best of my knowledge never went there.

Strangely enough, or maybe not that strangely, the first time I remember laughing at dementia was years after I left APS, and the victim was my mother. She had been diagnosed in 2012, and in her final years, she lived in an assisted living residence with a dedicated and highly competent 24-7 home health aide.

The aide, a 50-ish Trinidadian woman who was a sort of surrogate den mother to all the other working Trinidadian aides in the facility, had invited a bunch of her acolytes into my mom's one-bedroom apartment to celebrate her 94th birthday. There was a big birthday cake and plenty of good cheer.

"He probably won't shoot you"

The aides sat in clusters on the floor, talking about all the Trinidadian men with whom they had been amorous and the major romantic shortcomings of those men. The discussion got pretty raunchy. I looked over at my mother, who didn't appear to understand a word of what was being said.

Then, the birthday girl arose solemnly from her reclining chair.

"You know," she announced to the group, "I have never had sexual intercourse."

While the aides rolled all over the floor in hysterics, I explained to my mother that this assertion was patently false, given that she had conceived and birthed two children the old-fashioned way.

Anyway, my mother over her final years proved to be a rich font of gallows humor. She had always been at her funniest when she'd had one too many, so it was no surprise that as her cognitive abilities and inhibitions waned, she would come up with some real humdingers.

I discussed all this with a former APS case manager, now a supervisor, who concurred that client dementia was likewise not generally considered an appropriate source of amusement in her office. And yet, she added, sometimes the laughs pop up when they're least expected. The supervisor recalled one of the funniest of those cases.

Her elderly client had been plagued by dual diagnoses of dementia and urinary incontinence. The latter condition, however, had greatly improved with medication to relax her overactive bladder muscles; that is, until the client inexplicably began to once again pee all over herself whenever she set one foot in her bathroom doorway.

Her case manager asked the client about this backsliding behavior.

"Well," she replied, "I can't use the toilet if there's another woman in my bathroom, can I?"

"What do you mean, another woman?" inquired the worker.

"I mean the woman I see standing in there all the time who blocks my way whenever I try to go in," replied the client, referring to her own image in the full-length bathroom mirror.

"It's not a big bathroom," she added. "And that awful woman always gets there before I do."

I couldn't stifle a guilty laugh. Not a big one, but still, if a laugh is a fitting reaction to my own mother's demented bon mots, it ought to be fitting for a stranger.

If, in the afterlife, my laughter in this matter is judged otherwise, then, boy, am I gonna get yelled at.

CHAPTER 23

Celebrity Jeopardy

I've spent much, if not most, of my professional life in the presence of celebrities at the peaks of their careers, interviewing hundreds of pop music and film stars, literary lions, sports figures, journalists, barons of Wall Street, and prominent politicians, scientists, and intellectuals.

I got stoned with Freddie Mercury, swapped dirty jokes with Kurt Vonnegut, got cursed out by Lawrence Taylor in the New York Giants locker room, and was vilified by both George Harrison and Elton John (for radically different reasons). C. Northcote Parkinson laid out Parkinson's Law to me over lunch, and Benoit Mandelbrot, the polymath who pioneered fractal geometry, did his very best to explain his arcane theories to a mathematically-challenged reporter.

So, by the time I arrived at Adult Protective Services, I was past being overly smitten with the trappings of celebrity or the celebrities themselves (though I was not above a fan crush).

Over my time at APS, I encountered a fair number of the semi-famous and the almost-famous, this time on the flip side of their lives—living examples of the ancient showbiz axiom: Be careful how you treat people on your way up, as you'll be meeting them again on the way down. Once you've been referred to APS, you've already made that round-trip journey, all the way to the bottom. My job was to help these clients begin the arduous climb back up, if not to the top, at least to a reasonable facsimile of a good, healthy life.

I would not characterize my celebrity clients as being any more or less sad or dysfunctional than any others. They had fallen farther than most, and they had more interesting stories, more memorable memories. As a former journalist and a lifelong culture vulture, I reveled in their stories and tried to use them to build those archetypal bonds of trust that they teach you about on Day One of social work school. And while I was at it, maybe I could restore a bit of the dignity and luster that had been lost in the fall.

"He probably won't shoot you"

Emily, an elderly, ditzy lady living in a lower Manhattan one-bedroom, had been in her younger years a contract player in Hollywood. She was somewhere, I suppose, between a featured player and a bit player. Still, she always dressed the part of the ingénue, and on one particular visit, she was all dolled-up for a stroll on the red carpet.

"I don't have time to talk to you right now," Emily said, breathlessly. "I'm on my way to a friend's birthday party."

The friend, in this case, was a world-renowned, Academy Award-winning actress upon whom I'd had a crush for roughly 40 years. Emily had met her on the set of a film with Paul Newman in the early 1960s, and their friendship was a deep and lasting one. As for my crush, at that time it was still very much in force and remains so many years after the actress's death.

"Hey, I have a great idea!" my client effused. "Why don't you come to the party with me? I know [so-and-so] won't mind. I think she would really like you ... either way, it'll be fun."

A big part of me wanted to say yes, yes, yes, but the non-infatuated, non–Cinderella part of me knew this was a pipe dream. There could be no golden carriages, no glass slippers, for me. At least on this night.

First, there was my attire—APS crisis manager attire: blue jeans, sneakers, wrinkled sport shirt. Plus, I hadn't shaved in a couple of days, and, having made a particularly nasty home visit earlier that day, most likely I was just a teeny bit ripe.

Secondly, there was the small matter of the introduction.

"It's a pleasure to meet you," the evening's magnificent hostess would surely have greeted me. "How do you know Emily?"

"Uh, well, you see, I'm her crisis manager," I might well have stammered. "Emily's 17 months in rental arrears, and I'm trying to keep her from being tossed into the street. But I really love your work. You know, I once interviewed Joan Fontaine and she said Charles Boyer was her most generous leading man ... do you agree?"

Even by APS standards, this would have been a bizarre scene, and most likely worthy of job termination. Besides, if Emily's wealthy friend had learned of her unfortunate financial circumstances, she'd have cut her a $15,000 check right on the spot. Emily, if nothing else, was a proud and independent woman and would rather have died that night than accept her friend's charity.

On my next visit, I got the full rundown on the birthday party. Everyone who was anyone was there. Emily says she danced the night away, like Eliza Doolittle at age 80, reliving the grand ball. Emily and I

144

spent much of the visit schmoozing, as we normally did, the client sharing more lasting memories of the best years of her life.

Anyway, her eviction problem did get resolved—exactly how, I don't remember. I put Emily in touch with AARP to help her pay all her bills, manage her money, and get herself organized (her dining table was covered in giant piles of correspondence dating almost as far back as the Golden Age of Hollywood).

I closed her case with some reluctance, knowing I'd miss hearing about Paris in the springtime, and what Paul Newman, Julie Andrews, and Sidney Poitier were like when the cameras stopped rolling.

I'd seen a couple of Bernice's films and TV sitcom appearances, as I'm sure many of you have. In baseball parlance, Bernice was, way back in her day, what you would call a four-tool performer: actress, singer, dancer, comedienne, with a show-stopping smile and an endearing manner that made me like her right off the bat.

Bernice took great pride in what she had accomplished in her career, and she kept all those memories close at hand within a thick scrapbook, coming out of its bindings, that encompassed 50-plus years in "the biz": touring the globe, dancing with the stars, cementing lifelong friendships. She showed me the scrapbook on my initial visit, which I was able to thumb through after clearing the bedbugs from between the pages.

Bernice's fall from these heights to living alone in a bedbug-infested studio in a Manhattan rooming house spanned many years and many disillusionments, but was breathtaking all the same. She had outlived all her old friends and fellow performers, save one who lived hundreds of miles out of town and was not aware of Bernice's plight.

Bernice herself, by now in her mid–90s, was in moderate-stage dementia and not fully aware of the depths to which she had descended. But her long-term memory was still intact, and she would giggle like a schoolgirl when she remembered palling around with Cab Calloway on uptown Saturday nights and entertaining cheering audiences on Broadway and on luxury cruise ships.

Bernice's APS case had been referred by her landlord. It was clear that a heavy-duty cleaning and concomitant bedbug extermination were not going to solve her problems. She had reached the point where she could no longer live on her own and was in need of either 24 × 7 home care or placement in a nursing facility. In even the best of nursing homes, what was left of her mind—mostly her warm show biz memories and her gracious and engaging demeanor—would have been erased in short order.

But Bernice caught a break. Through that one remaining friend upstate, I learned that she had relatives living in the Midwest who might be willing to take her in. I phoned them up. They, too, were totally unaware of, and appalled by, the conditions under which Bernice had been living. But they wanted very much to have her come to Indiana to spend her remaining months, or years, in a clean environment, surrounded by people who cared about her. Bernice remembered these people fondly from all those years ago and was more than willing to accept their generous hospitality.

I had Bernice transferred temporarily to a nursing home rehab, where over a four-or five-week period, they managed to get her strong and stable enough to make the journey halfway across the country.

The day I brought her to JFK Airport and put her on the flight to Indianapolis was a day I won't soon forget. By the time we reached the terminal, Bernice was too weak to walk or even to stand, so I got her a wheelchair. There were long lines at baggage check-in and security. Back then, the tragic events of 9/11 were still very much on the minds of travelers and the people paid to protect them. As I recall, Bernice had only a long-expired driver's license, and no other valid form of ID (I suppose I should have checked all this out prior to departure).

In any event, the TSA, in its inimitable fashion, was insistent on making the air travel experience even more wearisome and deflating than necessary. Despite my entreaties to give a beaten-down and bewildered 96-year-old Broadway trouper the benefit of the doubt, they grilled her as they might a suspect from the no-fly list. They agreed to accept her ID but their magnanimity stopped short of the security checkpoint, where they pulled the poor old lady off the line and patted her down in her wheelchair. For a while there, I was not at all sure that they were going to allow Bernice to board the plane.

To my great relief, she and I survived the TSA experience and were admitted to the departure gate. I embraced Bernice and kissed her balding head, before she was wheeled onto the jetway. But before leaving, Bernice advised me that she had left her scrapbook behind in the rubble of her apartment and asked me to send it to her at her new address, along with her collection of antique coins, also left behind with the falling plaster and the bedbugs.

Once again, dressed in hazmat suit, goggles and gloves, I ventured into the House of Bedbugs and dug out the coins and the scrapbook. I thought I had brushed off all those vile critters before leaving the apartment, but as noted in other pages of this memoir, bedbugs are tricky little SOBs.

When I got back to the office and began packing up the scrapbook for mail delivery, a few of the critters emerged, scampering to the floor where I quickly stamped them out. I then proceeded to do a much more thorough inspection of Bernice's belongings, and my person, before bringing the package to the post office. Being embarrassed by my lack of appropriate bedbug hygiene, I said not a word to my fellow staffers. The fact that there was no subsequent bedbug outbreak suggests that I had not created a major problem in the office.

Bernice arrived safely at her destination and was warmly welcomed into the bosom of her extended family. I spoke to one of her cousins a couple of times over the next few weeks. She said Bernice was doing well, breathing that clean Middle American air and enjoying the company of all the little children in her new household. She said everybody got a big kick out of listening to Bernice narrate her career as it was illustrated in her scrapbook.

"She really did live an exciting life," the cousin said. "I'm glad she still has those wonderful memories."

Bernice died about six months later, surrounded by love, with memories intact and absent the bedbugs.

Another client with whom I very much enjoyed swapping tales, was a poet of only modest renown, but a first-rate raconteur, with a Runyanesque story about every colorful character south of 14th Street. She was as comfortable in the presence of Allen Ginsberg and William Burroughs as she was with leading members of organized crime.

"Chin was a sweet guy in some ways," she said of the notorious Genovese family mob boss Vincent "Chin" Gigante, with whom Eloise would occasionally hang out at a neighborhood social club. "I used to tell him all about my problems with my kids.... He once offered to straighten them out. I thought it prudent to politely turn down that offer."

I helped put in home care for Eloise, and while we waited for financial management to kick in, I made nice with her exasperated landlord, who was tiring of having to bird-dog the rent payments every month.

The fun part of this client engagement was listening to her stories and talking poetry. She shared some of her work with me, and I brought over a few of my poems, written many years earlier in a workshop at

New York University. She was gracious and supportive with both criticism and praise. I attempted to behave accordingly.

Other celebrity clients over the years included a well-known avant-garde composer, who was still making beautiful music at the time of the referral. Edward had worked with a few famous rock and roll musicians over the years, a couple of whom I had interviewed in a past life, so we had that to talk about.

Though his mind and spirit were willing, Edward's body was in steep decline, and he was in need of assistance with his activities of daily living. Placing this man in a nursing facility or adult home would have been nothing short of unconscionable. We put daily Medicaid home care in place, and Edward was able to remain safely in his home, with his piano and guitar, making his music, which he did for many years after his case was closed.

Still another client, a professional photographer of some note, was a friend of the legendary lensman David Douglas Duncan, who was as deft in his documentation of the epic battles of World War II and Korea as he was in the homes of Pablo Picasso, about whom Duncan produced seven extraordinary volumes of photojournalism. As it happens, my father, an amateur photographer and a fellow Picasso devotee, was also friendly with Dave Duncan, so this gave the client and myself a basis for conversation outside the mundane worker-client repartee.

The client had done a very slipshod job of marshaling his finances, and he was falling behind in his rent and needed home care. I facilitated a meeting of his family members, who jointly agreed to kick in a few hundred extra dollars a month toward the rent and obtained on the client's behalf a lifetime financial grant from a foundation that supports accomplished artists who have fallen on hard times. We also put in about 35 hours of weekly Medicaid home care, heavy-duty-cleaned the whole apartment and refurbished the living room.

I have no doubt whatsoever that I'd have performed the identical services with equal zeal for any client who had and no public profile and was not a buddy of my father's buddy. But, in some small, intimate way, helping out this guy carried extra weight.

Maybe all this effort was a nod to my old man, who had died a year or so earlier, or to every washed-out hoofer, wordsmith and visual artist looking for a little grace in the unlikeliest of places.

Adult Protective Services being one of those places.

CHAPTER 24

Tuesday in the Court with George

New York City's Housing Courts are where raw human dramas play out many times a day in the hallways and courtrooms. An ideal venue, one might imagine, for a daytime reality TV show. Just get someone as cantankerous and foreboding as Judge Judy and let the magistrate wail on deadbeat tenants or rapacious landlords for a half-hour every day.

Is that must-see TV, or what?

There are, of course, a number of very good reasons why no broadcast or cable network in its right mind would put *Housing Court* on its daytime docket.

For one, such a show would take a huge toll on law school admissions applications.

And then, there's this tiny slice of legal drama, which took place in Brooklyn Housing Court on an oppressive summer day about 10 years ago, with a slow-spinning ceiling fan stirring the miasma of stale air and desperation.

For Dorothy, the APS crisis manager, the day started off badly from the get-go. George, the client, a hoarder whose apartment had just undergone a heavy-duty cleaning that uncovered two dead canines and lots of other non-living things that were nearly as awful, was due in court for a hearing on his holdover eviction case.

"I was instructed to bring George to court in a cab, as he had failed to show up for his other appearances," notes Dorothy. "I help the man into the cab, and the driver says, 'Whoa, where did you get this guy from?' George did smell like he'd come out of a sewer, but the cabdriver was pretty cool about it, and we drove to court with the windows wide open and my head outside the cab, gasping for air."

When worker and client arrived at court, they found it crowded, as always. Mixed into the teeming throng in the hallway, the client's smells didn't stand out quite so much, but once they got into the narrow confines of the steaming courtroom, the client most definitely stood out, to the consternation of everyone in the general vicinity.

The judge, getting an initial whiff of George from all the way in the back of the room, barked, "What in the living hell is that?"

"It's my client, your honor," chirped Dorothy.

"Get that man up here right now!" ordered the judge, bypassing all the defendants at the head of the line. "Let's dispense with this case as quickly as possible and get this man home where he belongs."

The judge motioned to the case manager once they had approached the bench.

"I gotta tell you, they don't pay me enough for this," said the judge.

"No, your honor, they surely don't," replied the case manager. "Nobody gets paid enough for this."

Chapter 25

Terms of Endearment, or Disparagement

Here's a glossary of terms and acronyms that arise frequently in the daily maelstrom of APS life, with accompanying snark. Normally, a glossary appears at the end of the book, but this is APS, and I hate to go off-brand.

- **ACT Team, short for Assertive Community Treatment:** The team comprises a psychiatrist (or psychiatric nurse practitioner), a nurse, a social worker, mental health counselors, and support personnel. The aim is to deliver mobile, multidisciplinary services to at-home adults with primary mental health diagnoses who have fared poorly in traditional treatment (outpatient clinics, day treatment programs, etc.). I had a number of clients with ACT teams over the years, and from my admittedly limited perspective, the model tends to read better in print than it works in the field.

- **ADLs, short for Activities of Daily Living:** These are the seven basic tasks we all accomplish every day. They include bathing, grooming, dressing, feeding oneself, transferring, toileting, and ambulating. So-called **iADLs, or instrumental activities of daily living,** are those not deemed necessary for "functional living," but which allow individuals to live more independently in their communities and maintain a higher quality of life. iADLs include using a phone, meal preparation, housekeeping, laundry, shopping, managing medications, and handling personal finances. To qualify for private-pay home care reimbursement or Medicaid Home Care, the patient undergoes an assessment to measure his or her ability to perform all these tasks. The patient needs to show at least some level of difficulty with a number of chores in order to be eligible for home care insurance.

151

- **Article 81 Guardianship**: This article of law authorizes a court to appoint a guardian to manage the personal and/or financial affairs of a person deemed to be "incapacitated" (lacking the capacity to make decisions). Any family member, friend, or non-profit agency can petition the court on behalf of the individual. APS is the go-to source for clients who have no such support. In a nutshell, the process begins with a recommendation from a psychiatrist who must deem the client incapacitated. A referral by APS is then made to the city's Office of Legal Affairs (OLA), which, acting as APS's legal counsel, draws up the petition and represents APS in a subsequent court proceeding. Witnesses at Article 81 hearings generally include the APS worker, the psychiatrist and a court-appointed evaluator. I found testifying in these cases to be most unpleasant, especially before one particular Supreme Court judge, a curmudgeonly old buzzard whose behavior toward APS witnesses vacillated between grudging sufferance and malevolence. I just tried to keep my answers brief and on-point.
- **BPD, short for Borderline Personality Disorder:** Once the bane of APS workers and New York City psychiatrists alike, BPD is marked by long-term patterns of unstable relationships, a distorted sense of self, and wild mood swings. In recent years, mental health professionals have reported success in treating this disorder. I only wish those treatments were widely in place 15 years ago when my borderline clients were driving me to distraction.
- **Capacity:** Simply stated, it's the ability to take in information and use it to make and communicate a decision. Whether that decision is good or bad is irrelevant. How many smart, capable people do you know who do really stupid things on a frequent basis? It is possible for someone to lack capacity in some areas of life but maintain it in others. The head of thoracic surgery in the most prestigious hospital in the city may be hoarding rotting vegetables in his study. Moreover, capacity and incapacity may be permanent conditions or may come and go (for example, with or without psych medication). A few basic rules do apply: everyone is presumed from the start to possess capacity, and every step taken by mental health professionals should factor in the best interests of the patient and give the most weight to the "least restrictive option" in caring for that person. Like nearly all things related to APS, it's complicated.

- **CIU, short for Central Intake Unit:** All APS referrals are required to go through the CIU, either online or via telephone. But I've seen certain clients, those with a little clout, be able to direct their referrals to desired agencies or workers. I've phoned in a fair number of referrals since leaving APS, and some of the CIU operators I've encountered have presented as disdainful or stupefied. Amazingly, sometimes both at once.

- **Developmental Disability:** This is an impairment, distinguished from mental or physical illnesses. A developmental disability is a chronic condition which begins before age 22 and is likely to be life-long in duration. To be so classified in the state of Texas, which, as previously mentioned, has one of the most effective APS organizations in the country, the disability must materially hinder at least three everyday human functions (self-care, mobility, ability to communicate, etc.). The list of such conditions includes autism, Down's syndrome, fetal alcohol syndrome, cerebral palsy, attention-deficit/hyperactivity disorder, and Huntington's Chorea. My own experience in this field centered on getting clients into appropriate day programs or placing the neediest victims in long-term facilities specializing in the care of the developmentally disabled. A few of these cases lingered on well after closing. I remember one Huntington's patient, living alone in a ramshackle house and being unable to perform even the most basic personal care tasks. After placing the young man in a nursing home, I visited him for several weeks after, bringing him news of his beloved New York Yankees and trying to help him accept the loss of independence. I believe I still have a thank-you card from his brother, buried in a living room cabinet. It was the only APS memento I took home with me upon retirement.

- **Discharge Plan:** This is the plan for transitioning patient care from a hospital level to another level. It's supposed to be thorough and clearly understood by everyone involved, including the patients and their families. Above all, the plan is supposed to make sense. When it's a so-called "discharge to APS," quite often it doesn't, either because the patient is in no physical or mental condition to be sent back into the community, the client has been denied home care for being "difficult to serve," or the home environment is disgusting, hazardous, or (usually) both. In such situations, an APS director can respond with a Hospital Discharge Letter, an official request that the hospital postpone the scheduled discharge until all the necessary services are "reasonably available." Sometimes these urgent pleas work; more often, they fall on deaf ears. But, then at least they can't say that APS didn't give it the old college try.

• **DSM-5, short for the Diagnostic and Statistical Manual of Mental Disorder, Fifth Edition:** It's the principal authority for psychiatric diagnoses. Treatment recommendations, and health care provider payments, largely hinge on DSM classifications. The DSM-5 lists 157 specific psychiatric disorders, of which I must have dealt with at least 145 at APS. Explaining how the DSM-5 categorizes all these diagnoses would fill half this book. After reading the first few pages, you'll be inclined to take after Diogenes the Greek, setting forth across the land, with a lamp to light the way, in search of a sane person.

• **EDP, short for Emotionally Disturbed Person:** It's cop slang, with a loaded connotation: a subject who, as a result of severe mental illness or temporary derangement, represents a danger to himself (herself) or others. EDP cases are among the most challenging to police officers and require specialized training and enhanced de-escalation skills. I was fortunate, in this regard, to have worked almost exclusively with police officers who favored de-escalation over phony machismo posturing.

• **EISEP, short for Expanded In-home Services for the Elderly:** In New York, this is a state and locally funded program aimed at elderly (60 or above) people requiring personal care or housekeeping services, but too well-heeled to qualify for Medicaid and not sufficiently heeled to afford to pay privately for home-based care. Clients are required to share the cost of EISEP, based on a sliding scale that reflects their income and the full cost to the agency of the services provided. During my time at APS, seniors could get as much as 20 hours a week of EISEP. The last I heard, the maximum had been reduced to 12. By the time you read this, it may be even less.

• **Emancipated Minor:** This is a person under 18 who has the power and capacity of an adult. I have never actually encountered such an individual, professionally or personally, although I did once see this silly movie where Drew Barrymore emancipated herself from Ryan O'Neal and Shelley Long. I'm guessing in real life, emancipated minors are generally not anywhere near as cute and funny as Drew.

• **Emergency Medicaid:** This type of Medicaid covers emergency procedures for undocumented and "temporary" immigrant New Yorkers who otherwise qualify based on their low income. The laws in some states allow eligible recipients to sign up for pre-approval for the cost of future emergencies, but only for a period of up to 12 months. In New York State, one of the most magnanimous of the blue states, Emergency Medicaid and Adult Protective Services comprise basically the full extent of the social safety net for the undocumented. Keep that in mind the next time you hear a fellow American ranting about the millions of "illegals" taking government benefits away from red-blooded, taxpaying citizens. Because it just isn't so. All of us, as they say, are entitled to our own opinions, but not our own facts.

• **Emotional Abuse:** This is generally defined as language or behavior that serves no purpose other than to "intimidate, humiliate, frighten or harass" the one to whom these words and conduct are directed. It's a serious allegation, but it can be a difficult one for an APS worker to parse. I look at it this way. My nasty habit of back-seat driving when my wife's at the wheel— honey, you need to slow down, make the left here, don't hit the old lady—at times may constitute verbal harassment. But should my incessant hectoring cause her to seriously consider driving the vehicle over a cliff, with me still in the passenger seat, then it would most definitely be a matter for APS.

• **False Reports:** A person intentionally reporting information that he or she knows to be false or lacking factual foundation is, at least in some APS jurisdictions, guilty of a misdemeanor offense. I went out on a good many misdemeanors. I think they ought to be upgraded to felonies, but that's the APS in me talking.

• **Financial Exploitation:** Lone Star State APS defines this as the "illegal or improper use, or attempted use" of a client's resources, including his or her Social Security number and other identifying information, for monetary gain, without the informed consent of the alleged victim. The "informed consent" part is always a slippery slope. Many of these cases, in my experience, walked a tight line between what might be considered exploitation and just taking advantage of a situation. For example, there was a case I had of a pair of sisters in Canarsie, Brooklyn, who were paying a neighbor and his wife what seemed like an inordinate sum of money to run routine errands to the grocery store, drive them to occasional medical appointments, and help with a few household chores. The sisters, both pushing 90 and receiving several hours a day of EISEP home care, were clearly forgetful and maybe a bit daft, but they both could have easily passed their mini-mental exams. They allowed me to thumb through their checkbook and insisted that those payments—amounting to about $250 a week on average—were legit. They also showed me their wills, which left their house to the neighbor and his wife. The neighbor, meanwhile, got wind of my involvement and raised a ruckus, siccing his lawyer on me when I had a plumber come to the house to make a badly needed repair to a basement steam pipe. But here was the thing: the sisters had no family outside of each other, were both in excellent financial shape and in no danger of insolvency and seemed to like the man and his wife a great deal. I learned that years earlier, my clients and their neighbors had reached a verbal agreement—that in exchange for their support in helping the sisters remain safely in their home for the rest of their lives, the neighbors would inherit the house upon their deaths. So, perhaps the setup wasn't entirely kosher. But I couldn't find solid evidence of any deception or coercion, or a good reason to make a stink over it.

- **FMU, short for Financial Management Unit:** This is the name that New York APS rather pompously gives to its representative payee function. With a psychiatrist's recommendation, APS can arrange to receive the client's Social Security or SSI check, pay his or her essential monthly bills (rent, utilities, telephone) and disburse what is left over to the client. Generally, this applies to those mentally impaired clients with a history of not paying rent, and landlords who won't allow them to remain in their homes in the absence of a reputable payee. What they sometimes don't tell you is that an FMU client with a touch of the blarney can lay some sweet talk on a sympathetic Social Security clerk and have the process reversed. You could call this an empowering step for the client, but it's a great, big headache for the APS worker.
- **GAL, short for Guardian ad Litem:** GALs are appointed by Housing Court judges to advocate (free of charge) for tenants

facing eviction who are not mentally or physically able to advocate for themselves. Most GALs are lawyers, but the only real requirement for this gig is a pro bono heart (GALs with APS clients do receive a modest fee from the government) and a higher-than-normal tolerance for aggravation.

- **Holdover Eviction:** It's a housing court case in which a landlord is seeking to evict a tenant for a reason other than non-payment. Those reasons can be plentiful. Everything from being a "nuisance" to other tenants, staying on after the lease has expired, illegally allowing others to live in the apartment, or violating a term of the lease. A holdover action is more complicated than a run-of-the-mill non-payment case, which can be successfully resolved merely by paying the back rent. A holdover entails more detailed paperwork and shades of gray. For example, a landlord's attitude toward the tenant—and vice versa—can be significant factors. But should the tenant be on a month-to-month payment basis, pretty much any holdover eviction is "defenseless" on its face.

- **Immunity:** This applies to "authorized" workers conducting an investigation, testifying in court, or participating in any judicial proceeding arising from a petition, report, or said investigation. APS workers are immune from civil or criminal liability as long as they are acting in good faith. I did receive a few (meritless) legal and extralegal threats in my time at APS, but nothing ever came of any of them, no doubt a result of good faith and my faith in the power of goodness.

- **Intake Priorities for In-Home Investigations:** The priority level established at intake defines the time frames for beginning an investigation with an initial home visit and face-to-face interview. As best I recall, we had two priority levels in New York: a visit within 24 hours of receipt of the referral for "emergency" cases where clients were in danger of serious injury or death from physical abuse, lack of life-sustaining medications, sexual abuse, the elements (heat or cold), starvation, lack of critical care, and living conditions posing imminent safety or health risks; and 72 hours for all other referrals. Texas, by contrast, has established as many as four priority levels, ranging from immediate response to up to 14 calendar days. I would have liked to have been assigned some of those relaxing, 14 calendar-day cases.

- **Least Restrictive Alternative:** As in, always strive for.... In practice, it translates into not looking to place the client in a nursing home if all that's needed for his or her health and safety are 35 hours a week of home care. Or, not referring for a heavy-duty cleaning if all that's needed to make the home livable is a private-pay housekeeper with a broom and dustpan, a wet mop, and a can of Ajax.
- **Long-Term Care Ombudsman:** This is the person, or entity, charged with investigating allegations of maltreatment, neglect and other offenses against individuals residing in long-term care facilities. New York State APS does not deal with clients who live outside the community, but those state APS organizations that do work hand-in-hand with the ombudsman on cases that can curl your hair.
- **M11-q:** This is a request from a medical professional—doctor or nurse practitioner—for Medicaid Home Care (MA-HC). It is not an especially complicated form, which makes the M11-q something of an anomaly within the deep, black hole they call Medicaid. I've attended several Medicaid seminars and tutorials over the years, and I inevitably walk out with many more questions than answers.
- **Marshal's Notice:** In New York, this is the final step prior to the eviction itself. Once a judge has ruled in favor of a landlord's petition, the marshal is required to serve what is also called a "Notice of Eviction." The marshal must first attempt to serve it personally to the tenant or to someone of "suitable age" on the premises. If this is unsuccessful, the notice can be posted on the tenant's door or slipped under it. The marshal is then required to send copies within one day by certified *and* regular mail. The eviction may take place as soon as the 6th business day following the date on which the notice was mailed. There are more i's to dot and t's to cross, but my eyes are starting to glaze over....
- **Mini-Mental:** This is a major part of the standard psychiatric evaluation conducted by doctors from the Office of Mental Health. It's deemed to be a quick and effective way to ascertain a client's cognitive functioning and screen for cognitive loss. The mini-mental exam, among other aspects, tests for orientation in time (i.e., What is today's date?); place (What city are we in?); immediate and delayed verbal recall; attention (Count back by 7 from 100) and naming (Show the client a pencil and ask him

what it is). The test should take place in a quiet and well-lit room in the home, and the client should be attentive and at ease. But that's a rather high bar at APS. The top score on the mini-mental is 30. A score below 20 indicates cognitive impairment. Below 13 indicates a potential candidate for high elective office.

- **MMLTC, short for Medicaid Management Long-Term Care:** Under this arrangement, a state Medicaid program contracts with a single operator to provide all long-term care services for a set monthly fee. This is called a "capitation" plan. It's designed to save money by putting the risk on the provider. It may also incentivize said provider to cut back on services. Like everything else about the American health care system, it's, at best, a mixed bag, and quite often a bag of something else.

- **NAPSA, short for the National APS Association:** Founded in 1989, it is a non-profit 501 (c) (3) organization with APS members from all 50 states. Their primary mission is to encourage and facilitate information sharing among those 50 members for the purpose of improving their functionality. NAPSA also does research into such areas as worker training and client self-neglect, and they host an annual conference that brings the entire APS community together (or at least they used to do so pre–Covid). In seven years at APS, I was unaware of the organization's existence. In researching this book, I found NAPSA to be staffed by a spirited bunch of amiable and knowledgeable people who, as former workers themselves, feel their members' frustrations, but are perhaps more inclined to be sanguine about APS. Besides, they have plenty of old-fashioned APS horror stories of their own and the ability to find humor in them. I imagine the NAPSA annual conferences to be lively affairs, with free-flowing jocularity and ample inebriants.

- **NORC, short for a Naturally Occurring Retirement Community:** These are building complexes not originally designed for seniors, that over the years have seen many of their residents naturally age in place. NORC organizations offer these seniors a wide variety of services, including educational and recreational activities, supportive counseling, assistance with benefits and entitlements, transportation, and at-home nursing services. A NORC is one of the very few benefits of growing old, along with movie and subway fare discounts, and remembering how great rock & roll used to be.

- **NYCHA, short for New York City Housing Authority:**
  This state public development corporation was the first agency
  in the U.S. to provide housing to low- and moderate-income
  residents. Its 325 projects in the five boroughs house more than
  400,000 people, with another 235,000 or so receiving rent
  subsidies in private homes via Section 8. NYCHA apartments
  are notoriously hard to get. Once you're on the applicant list, it's
  strictly don't-call-us-we'll-call-you. Plenty of folks die waiting
  for their names to be called. NYCHA's been excoriated by just
  about everybody over the years—and much of that excoriation is
  justified—but I won't add to it here. I'll just note that providing
  clean and safe housing for 600,000 poor people in a city like
  New York is a tough job, and there are dedicated NYCHA
  employees in the field trying their damnedest to assist their
  tenants and collect the rent. I do wish, however, that one of
  them would have applied that dedication toward fixing a client's
  bathroom sink that gushed out a murky liquid substance for six
  months. I put in no less than four documented repair requests
  in that time, none of which received even a reply, let alone a
  plumber.
- **One-Shot Deal:** This is an emergency assistance grant from
  the city aimed at keeping tenants in their homes and reducing
  the growing numbers of people living in shelters and makeshift
  camps. To obtain a grant on behalf of a client, the APS worker
  must first prove that the client has the means of paying the
  rent and/or utilities going forward, and second, offer some
  reasonable guarantee that the money will be paid. This means
  FMU for those clients with SS/SSI. For others with no income,
  it generally means family members willing to take on the
  responsibility for ongoing payments. I personally obtained
  several one-shots in the $10,000 to $15,000 range, and have
  heard of others surpassing $20,000. If done correctly, a one-shot
  is considerably more cost-effective, and more socially beneficial,
  than what passes for homeless services in my fair city.
- **OSC, short for an Order to Show Cause:** A tenant on the verge
  of eviction has one last gasp at preventing it; getting a Housing
  Court judge to sign an OSC, which puts off the eviction until
  the tenant has a final opportunity to be heard in court. In most
  cases, the client needs to show two things to obtain such an
  order: a good excuse for not having shown up in court when

previously ordered to ("My dog ate the papers" won't cut it), and a good reason why the landlord shouldn't have prevailed in court ("My ceiling collapsed" or "The landlord wouldn't accept my rent check" would be sufficient answers). It's a long shot, at best, but an OSC can buy time for the client and case manager to figure out their next move.

- **Partial Day Program:** Patients released after a typically short stay in a hospital psychiatric unit—or, in some cases, an outpatient psych facility—often require additional structure to support their efforts to go back to their communities. A partial day program normally gives 20 hours a week (5 days × 4 hours) of individual and group therapy and other services for up to six weeks. I had many clients in such programs, and for those—a minority—who showed up for treatment every weekday, they seemed to do some good.

- **PCS, short for Purchased Client Services:** These are outlays that APS is able to make for client services such as emergency food or medical supplies, transportation, and housecleaning, when those services are not available through other local and state agencies. I fear that going forward post–Covid, this is the sort of essential client service that is going to be axed when those state budgets get sliced to ribbons. And that's a shame, because I made good use of those discretionary funds: for taxicabs to bring clients to the hospital for life-saving chemotherapy or dialysis; for temporary housekeeping help when a heavy-duty cleaning wasn't required; and to pay for needed home repairs.

- **RORA, short for Risk of Recidivism Assessment:** We didn't have this particular tool back in my day, and I'm generally not a big fan of these kinds of assessment vehicles. But in researching this book, I did come upon one study that showed as many as 60 percent of APS clients going into the system twice or more. Any data-driven tool that helps keep former clients former has my enthusiastic support.

- **Section 8:** No, not the piece of paper that would get Corporal Klinger back to Toledo. In New York, Section 8 is a housing program created in 1978 to provide rental subsidies to low- and moderate-income families. Clients receive vouchers enabling them to begin searching for apartments in the private market. They pay a portion of their adjusted monthly income toward the rent, and the New York City Housing Authority pays the rest. Two problems: many landlords are loath to rent to Section 8 tenants, and getting a Section 8 voucher in the first place is like getting a cheap Super Bowl ticket. I spent enough time on seemingly endless waiting lines with clients to testify as to the paucity of those precious bits of paper.

- **SHIELD, short for Strategies that Help Intervention and Evaluation Leading to Decisions:** Now, how's that for a mouthful? SHIELD is Texas-speak for a package of three distinct investigative tools which include the aforementioned RORA, a safety assessment, and a "strengths and needs" assessment. It's all too wonky for me, quite frankly, and I remember APS as being more freewheeling in both style and substance. I liked it like that.
- **SNAP, short for Supplemental Nutritional Assistance Program:** Better known as food stamps, SNAP is one of the most essential, and least fraud-prone, of all government services. It provides electronic cash benefits to low-income working people and their families, seniors, and the disabled for food purchases. Covered items include bread, fruit, veggies, meat, and dairy products. Booze, cigarettes, vitamins, restaurant food, and pet food are precluded. A major problem with SNAP is that not enough potentially eligible recipients know about it. Whose fault do you think that is?
- **SPMI, short for Severe and Persistent Mental Illness:** These are a group of mental illnesses that require ongoing treatment and are considered "disabling," in the sense that they cause "an extended impairment of functioning." These ailments include schizophrenia, major depression, bipolar disorder, and our old friend, borderline personality disorder. I would hazard a guess that more than two-thirds of my clients over the years had diagnosed, or in some cases undiagnosed, SPMI.
- **SSBCs, short for Social Security Block Grants:** This is the manner in which Congress chooses to allocate most federal funding to APS, among other social services entities. In the disbursement of those funds at the state level, APS over the years has been repeatedly shafted and would no doubt much prefer to receive the sorely-needed federal aid directly from Congress itself. Suffice it to say, in that regard, Capitol Hill has never been a fountain of generosity.
- **SSI and SSD, short for Supplementary Security Income and Social Security Disability:** Simply stated, the former is for the

162

aged and/or disabled who are very poor and unable to engage in any "gainful activity." In my day, the maximum amount of assets an SSI recipient could hold was about $2,000. In New York, if you share a two-bedroom apartment with a half-dozen people, limit your diet to rice and beans, and hop a lot of subway turnstiles, you can just about make it on SSI. SSD is for disabled individuals who worked long enough (usually 10 years) and paid substantially into the Social Security system. SSD puts no limit on accumulated wealth.

• **Termination of Tenancy**: This is the first step in a NYCHA eviction. In the end, NYCHA cannot evict a tenant without a Housing Court order, but those orders are far easier to get once NYCHA has won the termination proceeding. Tenants can lose their tenancy for a wide variety of reasons, ranging from "non-desirability" (someone in the household using, or dealing drugs, is a prime example); breach of the rules and regulations; chronic delinquency in rent payments; non-verifiable income and "misrepresentation" (lying about eligibility for admission or continued occupancy). If such a thing is possible, a day spent at NYCHA termination court, located at 250 Broadway in Manhattan, is even more demoralizing than one spent in the corridors of housing court. NYCHA court is generally mobbed with distraught and angry tenants, large numbers of crying children, and APS workers who would rather be anywhere else on earth. If a tenant can make a good case before the NYCHA hearing officer, he or she could remain at home with no conditions; be placed on a year's probation; be forced to permanently exclude an offending family member from the home; or be required to seek help from social services. A losing tenant has the right to appeal the NYCHA court decision in State Supreme Court within 4 months. This is called an Article 78 filing, and it is not often successful. I've assisted a handful of winning clients at 250 Broadway, but it's pretty hard when you're looking at all the sadness and desperation in the room to let that success go to your head.

• **Three-Day Notice**: This is step one of the eviction process: a note informing a tenant that if the rent is not paid within three days of receipt of the notice, an eviction proceeding will be forthcoming.

• **Thirty-Day Notice**: This is a notification of termination of tenancy, the last day of the notice being the last day of the rental period. It applies to tenants who have been renting their homes for a year or less. Sixty-day minimum deadlines apply to those with less than two years residency, and ninety days is the minimum for those residing in their homes for two years or more.

- **TPQY, Short for Third-Party Query Procedure:** This is a key form, enabling the APS worker to obtain proof of a client's Social Security/SSI benefits using his or her Social Security number. Income verification is a necessity in applying for almost any benefit or entitlement. In my day, we faxed TPQYs. Now the process is online and greatly streamlined.
- **Two P.C.:** This is shorthand for "two physicians certify." In New York State, one cannot be involuntarily committed to a psychiatric facility without being examined by two doctors who certify that the patient is in need of such care. Most of the clients I brought to the psych ward could have easily passed a 10 P.C. certification.
- **Vicarious Liability:** It sounds vaguely risqué, but it's not. The term applies to the responsibility that nursing homes and their contractors have for the abusive actions or neglectful behaviors of their employees. New York State APS does not investigate abuse or neglect outside the "community," but some programs around the country do. For those who have had family members mistreated in nursing homes, a horde of plaintiffs' attorneys fervently awaits your call.

Chapter 26

Nothing to It

Lest what you've read so far has cemented your view of APS as one long, commiserable slog through the minefields of despair, check out Juan's story.

Sometimes the job is just so damn easy.

From the outset of his case, it looked like this young man was going to be a lost cause. Juan, who was in his mid–20s, lived with his older brother in a Brooklyn housing project. The two brothers had recently lost their mother, and their sister, who lived somewhere else and had a family of her own, referred her siblings to APS because she was worried about their ability to adequately care for themselves now that their mom was gone.

Juan clearly had a significant developmental disability (defined as an IQ of about 70). He was a large, ungainly man, whose hirsuteness suggested long-term steroid use. He had dropped out of school many years before and had never held a job, had a friend of either gender, or engaged in much of any activity apart from sleeping, eating, and annoying his brother.

Juan spent nearly all of the first visit staring at me across the kitchen table like I was a visitor from another galaxy. He gave no indication that he had heard my casual suggestion that he consider enrolling in classes at a local jobs center that catered to the developmentally disabled. That center was roughly a mile and a half from his home but provided daily bus transport to and from.

Juan's brother appeared to be higher functioning and worked in a fast-food restaurant. Still, his housekeeping and culinary skills were minimal, and I spoke with the sister about hiring someone to come in once or twice a week to cook a few meals, run a vacuum, and do some laundry.

Anyway, I left the apartment that first day thinking I would make a concerted effort to get Juan into that jobs program or another similar program. Not only would it fill his time with purposeful activity, but

165

it would ensure he got nutritious meals every day and socialization with other young men and women like himself. The programs I had in mind also bundled in counseling and other social services.

Based on years of experience, I didn't envision Juan being at all receptive to such a program, and it would be a major coup just convincing him to allow me to bring him to the center for a visit.

At least that is what I thought.

When I returned to the home a couple of weeks later, Juan wasn't around. His brother told me that on the morning after my initial home visit, Juan had arisen at 6:30 a.m.—his normal wake-up time was closer to 11—and lumbered a mile and a half to register at the jobs center. He took all their tests, met all their criteria, and was admitted for training. His brother said Juan seemed to have found a "new home" there.

"He did this all on his own?" I said.

"Absolutely," said his brother. "I've never seen him like that. He's like a new person."

I arranged to meet up with Juan at the center. By this time, he had been placed in a job in their assembly operation, and he was loving it—piecing together plastic parts to create cheap baubles that the center sold in their retail outlet. The job came with a minimum wage salary, the first time in his life that Juan had received a paycheck. He loved that part, too. In fact, there wasn't anything about the whole setup that he didn't like. He had already made a slew of new friends and was in supportive therapy.

I recall asking Juan what had possessed him to finally take control of his life.

"You," he said. "It was you.... You told me I had to do something."

"No," I corrected him. "All I did was make a little suggestion."

Juan looked at me, dumbfounded. He was unfamiliar with the concept of suggestion.

Just a bit of a nudge had been enough to drive a man, who had heretofore displayed no discernible spark of ambition, to get out of bed and trudge forth into the world to make his mark.

Who woulda thunk it?

A year or so later, I brought another client to apply at the jobs center and bumped into Juan having a bite in the lunchroom. He had lost considerable weight by then, and had been promoted to a more responsible position in the assembly department. He seemed immensely, and rightfully, pleased with himself.

I made sure to let him know that I shared in that pleasure.

CHAPTER 27

Senior Lifesaving; Or, Hello, I Must Be Going

He who saves the life of one man saves the entire world.
—From the Talmud, the Koran,
and who knows how many other holy books

The list of clients I have had the great joy of rescuing from certain death is a short, but noteworthy, one.

Most of those on that list were in late stages of self-neglect. Such was the case with a morbidly-obese, diabetic, depressive in the Queens projects. The young man had disregarded all exhortations to see his cardiologist, until on one memorable visit, it became necessary to summon 911, and accompany the critically-ill client to the hospital, where he underwent a life-saving angioplasty. Or a woman in Brooklyn who hadn't seen her doctor since forever, and was complaining of terrible abdominal pain. I got her to the hospital in time to treat the most pressing ailment, but she passed away only months later from a thick stew of previously-untreated maladies.

Only two life-saving episodes in my experience did not comport with a self-neglect scenario. One was very weird and the other very sordid.

The first involved a male client in lower Manhattan and his roommate/lover. The referral, to the best of my recollection, featured no allegation of partner abuse or caregiver neglect, which made what happened on that visit all the more bizarre.

I arrived for the initial home visit around 9 a.m. and found the client lying half-naked on the living room carpet, trying to speak but generating only low, plaintive moans. His roommate was standing over him with an enigmatic expression that did not match these parlous circumstances. The roommate said the client had been complaining about pains in his chest, just before sliding off the sofa. He'd been lying there on the floor for some time, apparently.

"He probably won't shoot you"

"Did you call an ambulance?" I asked the roommate.

"No, should I have?" he responded.

And then it all got even stranger. The roommate, who was nattily dressed and carrying a leather briefcase, politely excused himself and headed for the door.

"I'm sorry to have to leave you like this, but I don't want to be late for work," he explained.

Before I had a chance to exclaim, "Are you serious?" the roommate was *solid* gone and I was left in the apartment with a stranger in desperate need of medical assistance. I dialed for the ambulance and waited for the paramedics, while the client continued moaning and grimacing. The moans were much welcomed, because as long as the man was making noises, his heart was still beating, and his respiratory system was still functioning, so an embattled APS case manager didn't have to put his long-forgotten CPR training to the test.

Funny, the little things you remember when you're waiting anxiously on an ambulance. There was a bowl of fruit on the counter of the kitchenette, and I thought for a brief moment about indulging in a large, juicy peach. But this incident was off the charts already without me making it more so.

At the hospital, the client went into the ICU, where he would remain for some time. As per APS guidelines on hospitalized clients, I closed his case.

But before I left the hospital later that afternoon, I was asked by the charge nurse about the client's home situation.

"Do you know if he has anyone at home who can care for him?" she inquired.

"He might have someone," I said, "but you have to catch him before he goes to work."

The second case also involved a significant other with some anomalous ideas about partnering.

The client here was a Guyanese American woman of about 55, suffering from end-stage renal failure and an unspecified, severe mental impairment, who was living with her husband in the Brooklyn projects. On my initial visit, the husband, a squirrely little man who hadn't held a job in years and was subsisting on his wife's Social Security income and handouts from his children, was hesitant about letting the client speak with me.

A classic red flag.

Whoever made the referral was concerned about the client's safety

168

in the home. As it happened, the referral source had very good reason to be concerned.

Armed with an APS case manager's sixth sense of Capital T trouble, I phoned up the client on a Wednesday afternoon, checking in on her when she was presumably back from her morning dialysis therapy. Her husband answered the phone. No, he said, she hadn't gone for dialysis on this day.

I immediately contacted the dialysis center and spoke with the medical director. He confirmed that the client hadn't shown up for treatment since the previous Monday. That's four missed sessions, the kind of compliance with dialysis treatment normally displayed by patients looking to commit suicide on the installment plan.

"It didn't bother you at all that your patient hasn't shown up for dialysis for the past week and a half?" I asked the doctor, incredulously. "Did you maybe think of calling 911?"

The doctor replied that, come to think of it, he hadn't given the matter much thought, so I went ahead and phoned for the ambulance. It arrived at the client's home within minutes, picked her up (against the husband's wishes) and whisked her away for emergency dialysis treatment.

The client somehow survived the missed sessions, and despite the opposition of her husband and, surprisingly, her grown children, she was placed in a nursing home after the dialysis center initiated guardianship proceedings.

The case never made any sense to me. If the husband needed his wife around for the rent money, why would he prevent her from getting life-saving care? And why were her children on the side of the perpetrator?

I never got the answers, but years later, I was advised that the client was still alive and residing safely and peacefully in the nursing facility. To a lot of people, maybe most people, a grim death is preferable to long-term placement in a nursing home. But, at least in this case, I do believe I did the client a service.

This life-saving thing, I thought back then, could become a habit with me.

The Supporting Cast

Adult Protective Services is a team sport. The cases are simply too complex and mystifying to be left solely at the discretion of overworked, overwhelmed, and underpaid underlings.

Thus, did God invent bosses and psychiatrists.

Program directors and supervisors, the majority of whom are former crisis managers with more ambition and something on the ball, in my time tended to exhibit a predilection for giving their workers the benefit of a doubt. As a group, I found them to be kind-hearted, empathetic, possessed of a strong sense of perspective and an ability to laugh when the world around them was crying.

Where the bosses largely differed was in how they approached the job, most notably, as regards the hiring function.

One former director I worked under for a relatively short period preferred to lay it all on the line right from the start, totally unconcerned that this level of candor might cause jittery candidates to excuse themselves from the interviews and bolt for the lavatory.

"I didn't believe in mincing words," he explains. "This is a high-pressure job and if you can't handle it in an interview, you're not going to last a day out there on the street. So, yeah, I would tell them upfront all about the malodorous situations they're going to encounter, the garbage piled from floor to ceiling, the crazies, the clients who will curse them out and spit on them, and the frustrations they're going to feel all the time....

"But I also made sure to tell them that the job gets easier once they've become acclimated to it, and there are supervisors and peers in the office who will support them up and down the line and help them get through the worst of it....

"And, if after relaying all that information, the applicant didn't run off screaming, then I knew I had a caseworker with spunk."

Another supervisor, to whom I reported for a much longer period, took an entirely different tack, which was to try a little tenderness.

Chapter 28. The Supporting Cast

"I remember how hard this job was for me when I started," she says. "The last thing I wanted to do in an interview was freak out the applicant. What I looked for back then was their experience ... had they faced adversity on their previous jobs? Did they appear to have the maturity, the patience, and the psychological makeup to do this kind of grueling work? Were they just looking for a job, in which case they'd be out of here the first time they got offered a better-paying one. And then, once they were onboard, we took it very slow for the first few weeks. I would send the [newbies] out with veteran workers, or, if I could, I'll go on home visits with them myself....

"I just think you've got to be very patient and understanding with all your people, especially on this job, and give them all the nurturing and support you can."

Another ex-boss said his hiring decisions at APS hinged on just three qualities.

"How resilient is the applicant? Can he or she get knocked down and get right back up quickly? How passionate and dedicated is the applicant toward helping people? I didn't want anyone whose major motivation was the weekly paycheck. And third, maybe most important, I looked hard for evidence of a well-developed sense of humor ... it could be dark humor, even a morbid humor. But if you're not laughing on this job, you're either a depressive or a sociopath."

Every boss I ever knew possessed an innate grasp of the enormous value of camaraderie, and actively encouraged workers to bond, through vehicles like "peer review" (workers getting together during business hours without bosses present to discuss their problems on the job and air their gripes). At least two of my old bosses were fond of strong drink and not only hosted regular after-hours gatherings in local bars, but actually picked up the tab, at least for the first couple of rounds.

As a former journalist and thereby a connoisseur in matters of free food and drink, I was much appreciative of this kind of largesse. And my colleagues, nearly all of whom were on limited household budgets, felt likewise obliged.

All APS bosses, then and now, feel the pinch of being wedged between the proverbial rock (lack of funding for staff) and the hard place (ever-rising caseloads). It's a perpetual no-win scenario.

"The hardest thing for me was dealing with constantly being short-staffed," says a former director. "This meant sometimes having to balance worker safety and well-being with all the other things that needed to get done to keep our funding intact and the operation going smoothly. There were times I would have much preferred to send two or three workers out on a difficult assignment, but I just couldn't spare the manpower....

"These are issues that came up every day, and I tried to deal with them by maintaining an open-door policy and making sure that I was being sensitive to input from my staff. Our staff meetings had a written agenda, sure, but there were always opportunities in those meetings for workers to speak their minds with the knowledge that I would take their concerns seriously."

Pressures also came from upstairs to keep the pipeline flowing. This meant wrapping up cases as quickly as possible to accommodate a backlog of fresh ones. At the APS units for which I toiled, we tended to play it faster-and-looser with those directives from on high. With the grudging imprimatur of my superiors, I kept some clients on my case-load for months, and in a few cases even years, after the initial problems had been resolved. This necessitated some fast shuffling on my part.

There was, for example, a sweet young woman of about 20 and her indolent boyfriend, who were facing eviction from their hovel, before the girl's parents broke down and took them in. The immediate problem solved, I was instructed to close the case. Instead, I wheedled a bit, dithered around, and employed additional stalling tactics in an effort to keep it open. My goal here was to convince the client—who had a mild developmental disability—to get treatment at a "day habilitation" program. Such a program, I believed, could have put the young lady on a path toward an independent life.

But this was APS, not George Bernard Shaw, and my would-be Pygmalion wasn't buying into my jaunty little narrative. She, too, dodged and feinted, before finally refusing to do anything but lounge around the house, knit sweaters and watch soap operas with her mother. Sadly, I had to give this one up and let the client be herself.

All these years later, my supervisor on that case and other similarly drawn-out ones, gently chides me for taking the job description of a crisis manager and twisting it to fit my wishful fantasies.

"I should never have let you get away with stringing out cases like that," she says now. "You know, you really did take advantage of my good nature."

The psychiatrists whose medical opinions determined the course of action on so many of our cases were similarly-indispensable allies in the war against dysfunction. They went out with us into those horrendous environments, suffered the same frontal assaults on their senses, and tamped down the same fears and trepidations.

But they were doctors, and tended to maintain a more dignified bearing on the job, as befits a profession that dates back 2,500 years to the Age of Pericles. This was reflected in their more businesslike home visit attire—jackets and ties for the guys, pant suits for the gals.

"Generally, we got more respect from clients than [did] their APS workers," says one psychiatrist. "I think that's just the nature of a doctor-patient relationship."

The docs also tended to take a less ironic view of the vast divergence between what should happen on a case and what actually happens.

The psychiatrists at the New York State Office of Mental Health had their own culture and their own set of frustrations.

One of those was not being able to follow up after their evaluations or witness the outcomes of the cases, especially the most interesting and distressing ones.

"Unlike you and your APS colleagues, unless I was subsequently called into court to testify in a guardianship matter or in housing court, or the client's situation deteriorated to the point that I needed to conduct a second evaluation, my involvement ended with the filing of the initial report," notes Dr. Lewis, a now-retired OMH psychiatrist who impressed me over the years with her equanimity under stress.

"And, even if I'd been able to stay in touch with the progress of a case, there was simply no time to go back. We usually had multiple visits scheduled every day, finish one interview and move on to the next.... I found this feeling [of incompletion] to be one of the least appealing aspects of the job."

Dr. Lewis says she has never held any illusions about her limited involvement in this daily drama of human suffering.

"The reality is that in a huge percentage of these cases, there *are* no good solutions," says the doctor. "In my mind, if nothing else, what I accomplished with these patients was better than nothing."

To be fair, my discussion with Dr. Lewis occurred during the first weeks of the Covid-19 outbreak, when nobody in the known world was feeling good about anything. So her lackluster summarization of her OMH career should be viewed skeptically.

As to her opinion of New York City APS, having accompanied hundreds of case managers in the field, Dr. Lewis is less than fulsome in her praise.

"Some of the workers were okay, but a lot of them were not

well-trained or well-informed about their clients," she says. "And there were some who didn't seem to really care about them all that much … but, in their defense, they were all managing big caseloads with a lot of unstable clients.

"Still, when I did go out with a caring worker with an educational background in the humanities, who could add context to the situation, it made a definite difference."

Just as case managers come in all shapes, sizes, and personalities, so, too, did these imperturbable practitioners of the healing arts. Even within the boundaries of a routine psych evaluation, those personalities emerged in unusual and striking ways.

Dr. Dennison, for example, was an odd duck who found it useful with certain female clients to combine cosmetology and psychology. On several visits, I watched her cut my clients' hair, zeroing in on those clients least likely to have had a professional beauty treatment in the recent past.

First, she would make the clients comfortable in their chairs, before taking on the thick and tangled masses of matted hair with a wide-toothed comb. Just combing through the mess of entanglements could take 20 minutes or more. Then she'd apply the shampoo, break out a pair of scissors, and start joyously trimming away.

The clients, for their part, seemed to enjoy this kind of attention, certainly more than they did submitting to the psychiatric evaluation. Watching Dr. Dennison perform her cosmetological feats of magic, I came to understand a little better what makes women the world over so enamored of their hairdressers.

Dr. Baum was another odd duck who drove a German automobile about the size of a large suitcase, and revitalized the occasionally dull routine of a psych evaluation with musings that ranged from the merely incongruous to the preposterous. He spent some time on one visit getting me to consider that the World Trade Center attack was an inside job.

Nevertheless, these odd ducks, and all the other psychiatrists with eccentricities of their own, were also knowledgeable, insightful, and thoroughly professional in their conduct.

Generally speaking, they were the kind of companions a case manager needs when adrift in a boundary-less Sargasso Sea of crazy.

CHAPTER 29

Scammer's Delight

Sometime in the late 1980s, a group of friends and I visited another friend who was living with his wife and a half-dozen or so kids—several from his first marriage, the rest from her first—in a cramped, grimy railroad flat in the East Village. We adults were huddled around each other in the bedroom when I inquired as to the whereabouts of the children.

"Hey, kids," the father called out. "Come out and meet our friends!"

And with that, a gaggle of grade schoolers, toddlers, and rug rats exploded out of the two bedroom closets like passengers from a clown car.

Millions of New Yorkers have at one time or another experienced life in extremely tight spaces—my ex-wife and I once hosted a birthday bash for over 100 guests in our studio apartment. But this apartment was the cover story in Better Claustrophobic Homes and Gardens. I remember marveling at the cleverness with which Arthur and his wife had tricked-out those walk-in closets with narrow bunk beds and track lighting.

Anyway, we all had a good laugh about a bus driver's family living in a nursery rhyme, and then took all the children out of that shoe for some ice cream, mostly to stretch our legs and breathe some oxygenated air.

Walking into Florence's NYCHA apartment for the first time flashed me back to Arthur and the closet kids. Her children—at least five, by my count—may not have been stashed in poky spaces, but they were no less exuberant, gleefully and carelessly bouncing out of their bedrooms, knocking items off tables and otherwise making a giant mess of things.

Florence, like Arthur, took such hijinks in stride, as she did most matters, including her health (very poor), her rent (unpaid), and her reputation among NYCHA staff as one of the most problematic tenants in the entire building complex.

As regards her checkered history of rent payments, the issue that brought me into her life in the first place, if you were to plot those payments on a graph, it would resemble the EKG of a very arrhythmic heart. One month paid, two months off, another month paid, three months off. And like that....

Florence herself had been denied Supplemental Security Income (SSI) by a judge at a hearing, despite authenticated diagnoses of morbid obesity, diabetes, partial blindness, and the applicant's use of a wheelchair. But even without her income, there was ample money coming into the home to cover the rent and all the monthly bills—the kids were all collecting either Social Security Disability or SSI. It's just that Florence had other plans for that money.

Like spending it on lots of cool stuff.

A living room set and a new dining table, new mattresses for all the kids, and a spanking new refrigerator. All purchases she might have been able to afford had she made them one at a time with money saved in a cookie jar. But Florence preferred those ever-popular layaway plans that, if they were ever to be fully paid off, would have cost Florence thousands more than if she were to simply buy all those household goods outright.

I sat down one afternoon and explained this to the client; that she could buy the living room set for $700 but buying it over time would ultimately cost her more than $3000, provided the layaway loan was ever to be fully repaid, with Florence then taking final possession of the goods. Of course, none of her loans ever got repaid, and in the end all the cool stuff in the apartment was repoed, returning to the place whence it came.

Florence had no aptitude for, or interest in, these subtleties of home economics.

That, and a fleeting relationship with reality, made her an easy mark for all the unscrupulous retailers, phony charities, and for-profit college fraudsters preying on the elderly and infirm.

The college hustle was, to my mind, the most egregious. Still prevalent today, the success of the swindle hinges on the recruitment of gullible, low-income individuals who are encouraged to take on enormous levels of federal government-backed student debt before they're enrolled in courses they will never take if they live to be a thousand years old.

Florence's recruiter signed her up in a jiffy, giving her the old song-and-dance about a college education leading to a high-paying career. That, and the fact she'd never have to pay back Uncle Sam, were all it took to seal the deal. The recruiter assisted Florence in filling out the paperwork, which she proudly showed me on a home visit. She was brimming with the confidence common to victims of a fictitious American Dream.

"Isn't it great?" said Florence. "I never believed I'd end up in college."

Of course, Florence would be getting no closer to college than I would to the moon. The closest she would get to an educational experience would be me explaining to her the many unpleasant side effects of the layaway.

As expected, spring semester at Scam University got underway without Florence in attendance. Uncle Sam, for his part, ate about twenty grand in student debt, and Florence's credit rating, not very high to begin with, skidded all the way to zero.

On the positive side, she would be getting food stamps and 40 hours-a-week of Medicaid Home Care that APS put in place to help her with housekeeping, bathing, meal preparation, and other tasks. Article 81 guardians, appointed for Florence and her children, would eventually steady the spasmodic stream of rental payments, thus resolving those eviction concerns.

As for all the scammers out there in Scam Land, they now had one less target.

All of this was to the good.

But not all my clients were quite as fortunate as Florence. Some with big hearts and cash on hand lost their meager savings to non-existent charities; others fell victim to the ubiquitous mortgage fraud that nearly sank the global economy back in 2008. Most often, by the time I was made aware of these fiscal shenanigans and was able to bring them to the attention of the local District Attorney's office, the money was already dead and gone, to somewhere in Nigeria or the Gold Coast of Florida.

Some of the oldest varieties of con never die. As a senior citizen myself, I still get the occasional call from a phony Police Benevolent Fund, or boiler-room operators hawking worthless storefront stocks. But a new generation of slick hustlers have concocted bold, new swindles employing sophisticated technologies, enabling them to target more people in less time, and thus rake in more ill-gotten gains.

New-and-improved chiseling technology has no doubt been vexing for today's APS case managers, because, through all these technological changes, there remains one constant:

APS as a never-ending, primary source of fresh victims.

CHAPTER 30

How'd I Get Here?

At Alcoholics Anonymous meetings—I've attended some in support of friends in recovery—you hear those archetypal stories, alternately funny and sad, about waking up after a bender and finding oneself in a strange place. Like a men's room in Las Vegas, a cheap motel in Tijuana, or, more likely, a dumpster behind a Walmart in East McKeesport, Pennsylvania.

There's never an explanation given as to how they got there, as that would negate the point of these stories, which is the chaos that's brought about by terrible choices, and the courage it takes to get up in front of a room full of strangers and tell them out loud.

I've met APS workers in somewhat similar straits. They're the ones with the perpetual expression of bewilderment; the look that seems to ask, *What crime or misdemeanor must I have committed in a past life to wind up in a Salvador Dali painting?*

I confess to putting on that face at various times, especially when gazing upon a client's surrealistic wallpaper design that, upon closer examination, revealed itself to be nothing but a mottled congregation of cockroaches.

What sorts of people, of their own free will, choose this line of endeavor? Did they get here on a bet, or at the tail end of a bender? What motivates them to come to APS in the first place, and, more important, what drives them to stay after they've seen the cockroach wallpaper?

I've seen them come from all walks of life, from all social backgrounds, and all rungs of the financial ladder. Some took to the job right away; others never did or ever could. APS case managers, at least in my home town of New York City, appear to have little in common, aside from being a bit cuckoo.

These are their stories:

"It was the sheer desperation for money that brought me here," relates Deborah, a long-time case manager and supervisor, now happily retired. "I was working for a corporation that went bankrupt all of a sudden, with no notice. So here I was, a single mother with a son in college and no way to pay his tuition for the next semester. I needed another job right away, and I didn't have a whole lot of options at that time.

"I'd worked in social services before, but I had no idea what Adult Protective Services was all about when I accepted the job, only that the pay sucked even more than most social services jobs and most of the people in the office looked stressed out. The good part was that the program director was flexible and my co-workers all seemed to be nice people....

"I told the director I knew how to do case management, so he sends me out alone on my first day on a hoarding case. I knew nothing about hoarding and this was a really bad case. I didn't think I would survive the week."

What kept Deborah coming back for years to come was the creative challenge of helping people, many, if not most, of whom didn't want to be helped.

"What I loved about this job was that every day was different, and you never knew when you woke up in the morning and came into work what you were going to experience that day.... I found it exciting and fascinating back then. I can't honestly say I miss it now, but those old memories are good."

Deborah's APS origin story mirrors that of many young women with whom I worked: single or divorced moms, needing to support their families and giving little thought at first to what APS work actually entails. A few of these women lasted years on the job, eventually rising to management positions. Most others passed through on the road to nursing school or a Master's in Business Administration.

"I never much liked the work," says Aurora, a married mom who made a pit stop at APS for a year or so before moving on to a better-paying job in the healthcare field. "Yes, we had fun times, and my colleagues were great. I even liked most of my clients. I'll remember and talk about my APS experiences for the rest of my life. But it was never my career goal and I'm glad to be out of it."

Louisa, who likewise stayed on for a few years before leaving for a more lucrative opportunity in public school administration, says her APS years were memorable ones. They were mostly fond memories, she related over the phone, but some most un-fond.

"But you know, now that you bring it up," she added, "I don't think

"He probably won't shoot you"

I want to talk to you about those experiences. No, I think I'm going to write a book of my own."

Here's wishing her good luck with all that.

Oscar, meanwhile, came to APS from the upper echelons of Wall Street, where he had accumulated a considerable nest egg and a desire not to spend any more precious time around other Wall Street executives. Oscar brought to the case manager job not only organizational expertise and time management skills, but also an empathy for the disadvantaged, garnered from a lifetime of volunteer work with psychiatric patients, people with HIV, and others with bodies and souls in torment.

His Buddhist faith and a near-death experience in his youth contributed to Oscar's world view—one that encompassed more than a healthy 401(k).

"I thought APS was a good place to apply all those spiritual lessons," he says.

Oscar's forte, if an APS case manager can be said to have a forte, was calming desperate people in the throes of full-scale meltdowns. He was at his very best when applying those soothing powers to decompensating clients amid the madness of a waiting room in a county hospital psych ward.

And, finally, there were all those who just sort of fell into the job, and remained there in a daze from the day they arrived to the day they departed. This group included those lacking the mental acuity or temperate disposition to handle the huge workload; and, I'm sorry to say, those case managers who should have been referring themselves for protective services.

Case in point was the gentleman who had my job before me. As noted in Chapter 3, he was less than diligent about making his monthly home visits but extremely consistent when it came to lying about it to his supervisors. All that, and his habit of bringing hookers into the office after hours, and leaving the used condoms behind as souvenirs for his office mate, ultimately led to his inglorious exit from APS.

I guess you could say that it was those illicit assignations and prophylactics that paved my way to a career at Adult Protective Services.

And what more appropriate paving stones could there be for such a career?

CHAPTER 31

Change Is Gonna Come

Man plans, God laughs.
—Old Yiddish saying, and the title
of Public Enemy's 13th studio album

Writing this chapter, attempting to speculate on the many large and small changes that will affect the workings of APS in the wake of a global pandemic, is close to being an impossible task. What I type today is likely to be obsolete by next Thursday. This is the world in which Adult Protective Services finds itself: the most wildly uncertain times I can recall in my 72 years of existence.

There is currently no national, or global, consensus on where the human race goes from here. To date, Covid has claimed thousands of lives just within the two square-mile confines of my neighborhood in northwest Queens.

So, having been introduced to the mad, mad, mad world of Adult Protective Services in the pages of this text, and knowing it as you do now, you would likely assume that APS is as clueless about its future as is any other organization, if not more so.

And your assumption would be correct.

"We talk constantly about where we're headed down the road," acknowledges NAPSA executive director Lori Delagrammatikas, "but that's a hard thing to do when you're staring into a big, black hole."

The daily swirl of new information (and misinformation) has overrun the ability of any social service agency to plan past the next day. A "socially-distanced Adult Protective Services" would appear, on the surface, as classically oxymoronic as a deafening silence or a definite maybe.

Nevertheless, adds the NAPSA official, there are developments looming on the horizon that one can glimpse even through the pitched darkness of a black hole. Those developments will dramatically impact APS on multiple levels. For our purposes, let's examine just three: finances, organization, and culture.

"He probably won't shoot you"

As regards the financial outlook:

It is inevitable that whatever the extent of the economic recovery once a vaccine is widely available and more people return to work and start spending their income, every government-funded social service entity is going to have to learn to do more with less. It's no secret that APS has been operating in this vein since its inception, as evidenced in the depressing history enumerated in Chapter 2.

But the Covid-19 phenomenon has brought this already desperate situation to new levels. The immense budgetary gaps that every American town, city, county, and state will face over the coming months and years will very likely exact a terrible toll on America's underfunded and frayed social safety infrastructure. And, as you've been following this story all along, you know where APS ranks in the safety net hierarchy—at, or dangerously near, rock bottom on the budgetary priority list.

During the early stages of the pandemic, most state APS agencies have either frozen hiring or begun letting their people go, coming in the midst of a tidal wave of new cases stemming from the crisis. These are sure to include elder and spousal abuse cases that have been playing out quietly behind closed doors, but will doubtless rise in number as the nation opens up and victims emerge into the light. It is reasonable to expect many more cases of caregiver neglect and self-neglect in the form of non-compliance with medical treatment and medications, and, most notably, at least here in New York City, a veritable flood of evictions once the moratorium on them has been lifted and landlords, starved for cash to pay their mortgages and real estate taxes, go back on the offensive.

"I can't imagine how this will go with fewer workers and more clients," says a former APS program manager. "Just in terms of managing workloads. A worker in New York with, say, a caseload of 35, is mandated to see every one of those clients once a month, which is difficult enough when they're not home and you have to keep going back again and again until you find them. On top of that, many clients require multiple visits in a single month. I had people with no income who needed help with getting Public Assistance, or what they used to call 'welfare.' This is a slow process that usually requires at least several trips to the local welfare office. How does a worker find the time to escort a client to all those appointments, possibly sit and wait there for hours on end, and still find the time or the energy to make all the other mandatory monthly visits? I suspect some of the old rules are going to have to change. Otherwise, it's ludicrous...."

182

Chapter 31. Change Is Gonna Come

Add to this fewer dollars to cover transportation and other routine costs, and the short- and long-term financial prognosis would appear to be bearish at best, cataclysmic at worst.

On an organizational level, observers envision the pandemic ushering in substantial changes in APS daily functioning. It is already hopping aboard the virtual bandwagon.

A logical question is how an organization that relies so heavily on the ability of an individual case manager to make human connections based on building trust with skeptical or blatantly hostile clients is going to manage this awesome task remotely.

It's a question for which there are no answers, at least none at the present time.

"There are a number of states right now which are conducting their APS investigations solely by telephone," notes Delagrammatikas. "And those that are still making home visits are being a lot more circumspect about how they manage them."

Field workers, especially the dedicated ones, naturally hate operating in this fashion, not just because it takes much of the human touch out of the equation, but just as importantly, drastically reduces contact with colleagues and supervisors.

"We simply have to be more flexible to work around the obvious limitations," says an APS program manager in a Midwestern state who requested the state not be identified, as our brief conversation occurred outside bureaucratic lines. APS field workers there did not go on any home visits for the first 10 or 12 weeks of the pandemic, but are now going out into the community, cautiously and selectively.

For example, workers are now being given the flexibility of deciding which clients they are comfortable visiting, and which need to be followed in some other ways.

"In those cases, we will have to rely on more contact with collaterals and having our clients under the eyes of law enforcement," says the manager. "It's going to be very fluid, and full of uncertainty."

This state's long-term plan further calls for the closing ofbrick-and-mortar offices, with workers operating out of their homes and employing "hoteling options" when traveling to more distant locations. Abandoning headquarters as a means of reducing overhead is a difficult discussion that's currently taking place in dozens of APS organizations across the country. Some states have already made that hard decision; others remain uncommitted but are leaning strongly in that direction.

In more rural areas, where workers are already spread thin across large catchment areas, infrequent visits to HQ represent one of the few, if only, opportunities for them to bond in solidarity, commiserate with each other, and share their laughter.

This is a fundamental cultural component that truly separates APS from other social services like Meals on Wheels or "friendly visitor" programs. All very nice and tidy, but relatively sane. I've worked in both worlds, and I can tell you that no MOW client has ever forced me to engage in a wrestling match or asked me to carry three large bags of empty beer cans to the supermarket to reclaim the 5-cent deposit. Few have made me laugh out loud at the vicissitudes of human life spent on the margins, and even fewer have caused me to seek out my peers for advice, confirmation, and consolation over a cold brew.

"We're cognizant of the huge cultural impact [that isolation] is going to have on our workers," says the Midwest director. "We're trying our best to deal with it through more frequent Zooming, among other things."

And, lastly, there is yet another cultural change afoot, as regards the traditionally close relationship between APS and law enforcement in many jurisdictions. This relationship is already coming under great strain in a time of Black Lives Matter. APS officials in Minneapolis have forcefully addressed this matter, following the death of George Floyd at the hands of—or rather, the knees of—the very people pledged to protect him.

No doubt, some states will manage these transmutations more seamlessly, and successfully, than will others. But no matter how they all wind up slicing and dicing it, the New Order of Things will be a painful and grinding one.

Perhaps the perfect word to describe all this—the *mot juste*— is a Naval term my dad picked up from the sailors who deposited his 125-pound sergeant's carcass on Iwo Jima in March 1945. Dad passed it along many years later to his only son when the boy came of age.

The word is *clusterf—k*.

CHAPTER 32

Officious Channels

Amid the surrealistic mayhem that defines so much of life at APS, one is prone to overlook the fact that it is also a cog in the maze-like machinery of state government. And, as such, it has its administrative procedures, levers of command and control, and punctilios.

As a worker, I was well aware of my status as a cog within a cog, but I didn't spend much mental energy cogitating on it, because, as previously stated, I was too busy tiptoeing through debris and chasing down unscrupulous gypsies.

In completing research for this book, the bureaucratic side of Adult Protective Services reared its inhospitable face.

I had wanted to include a chapter toward the end that would explore the insights, feelings, and frustrations of today's APS crisis managers; the aim here being to compare their experiences with my own and with those of others who have long opted out of the adult protection business. And, further, to get some sense of what it's like to simultaneously navigate clients' needs and manage the health risks of Covid-19.

I reached out to approximately 15 state and county APS organizations, from the eastern shore of Long Island to the rocky coast of Northern California, requesting brief interviews with their current workers. I promised anonymity to any worker willing to speak with me, and further gave assurances that no clients or locations would be named in the book.

I got stonewalled.

"Owing to the many demands put upon our staff, we cannot accede to your request at this time," wrote back one state public affairs coordinator, in pitch-perfect bureaucratese.

Nevertheless, I thought it pertinent to give at least some sense of what today's APS crisis managers are facing out there on the streets. So I did the next best thing, turning to a long-time friend and mobile crisis worker in upstate New York.

"He probably won't shoot you"

After the state locked down back in March 2020, Miranda, sedulously and selflessly, continued to make daily home visits through the end of May, eventually stepping away due to some personal family and medical issues.

For her "essential service" during the first fearful, trying months of the pandemic, her agency rewarded her with a $25 cash bonus.

The nature of Miranda's job fairly closely mirrors that of an APS case manager, only with somewhat more accommodating clients and considerably less garbage.

"Making visits during those first few months was weird and very scary," she says. "First, there was all the PPE [personal protective equipment], which you had to change into outside the client's front door before you could enter the home. I wore two masks, an N95 mask *and* a surgical mask, a shield, gloves, and a ginormous one-size-fits-all jump suit that was four sizes too big for me.

"I can't imagine what my clients, especially those who just came out of the hospital or rehab and were terrified themselves about catching Covid-19, must have thought about having a team of social workers, nurses, and physical therapists coming in who looked like space aliens. Verbally communicating with clients through all that gear was also awkward, and in homes where the thermostat was turned up and it was so darn hot, my glasses would fog up and I could barely see who I was talking to."

Miranda says she had to bring in her own seat if she wanted to sit during the interview and took all her notes on a computer tablet wrapped up in a plastic bag. And, when the visit was over, she adds, there was the matter of carefully taking off all the PPE on the front lawn and depositing it safely in another plastic bag, before heading off to the next visit and repeating the same routine all over again.

"This job has been a big part of my life for the past 25 years and I love my clients," notes Miranda, "but, I have to say, this was asking an awful lot for 25 bucks."

She hopes to return to work once society returns to something approaching the old normal. But what will social services fieldwork look like in the new, old normal?

"I'd rather not think about that right now," says Miranda.

CHAPTER 33

Journey's End

Dere's no guy livin' dat knows Brooklyn t'roo an' t'roo,
because it'd take a guy a lifetime just to find his way
aroun' duh goddam town.
—Thomas Wolfe, "Only the Dead Know Brooklyn"

Tell me about it, Thomas.

It was June 3, 2010.

Maybe I'm off by a couple of days, or even a week. It doesn't matter. For the typical APS crisis manager, if there is such a thing, it often seems to come down to the one day when you realize you've had it. When your body, your mind, or both, tell you it's time to move on.

June 3 was a stultifying late spring day in downtown Brooklyn, 103 degrees, according to the meteorologists. Waves of heat shimmered atop the sidewalks, and the humidity weighed heavily on my 62-year-old shoulders, causing me to walk with a forward slouch. There was nowhere to hide to escape the glare of the sun.

"...Canarsie an' East Noo Yawk an' Flatbush, Bensenhoist,
Sout' Brooklyn, duh Heights, Bay Ridge, Greenpoint—duh
whole goddam layout, he's got it right deh or duh map."
"You been to any of dose places," I says.
"Sure," he says. "I been to most of 'em."

On June 3, 2010, I had no fewer than three home visits that needed to be made by day's end, and they were spread geographically across the vast expanse of the Goddam Borough of Brooklyn. There was a 19-year-old gay man, a new client, reporting abuse by a homophobic roommate in an apartment near the Brooklyn Museum. A female client in the projects near Avenue Z and Nostrand Avenue had run out of food and psych meds. And even with all her meds and a full refrigerator, she wasn't faring all that great. And, lastly, a client on the outer fringes of Coney Island was reportedly being hassled by her landlord, and just this very day threatened with eviction, due to the messes left in the building by her incontinent terrier.

I took out my subway map and studied it. This was going to require some logistical planning.

On the crowded subway platform at the Jay Street station, the temperature was running close to 110 and before I had piled into the train to make my first visit of the morning, my shirt was glued to my chest. I think it was in the oppressive swelter of the underground where I had my initial thought of leaving APS forever.

But it's never just about the heat or the humidity. There was a spike in new referrals that week that witnessed my caseload jump to 45. That's a client list nearly as long as Bernie Madoff's rap sheet and virtually impossible to service. For the record, a caseload of 45 translates to 10 or 11 home visits a week, assuming that all those clients happen to be at home when you show up.

"This is completely insane," I told my supervisor, a gentleman possessed of great patience in most respects, but not when it came to gross insubordination.

I was pretty worked up and almost out of control.

"When I started here in 2004, we had maximum caseloads of 30, maybe 31 or 32, tops ... nobody can handle a caseload this big, unless all the cases are stable, and that has never happened before in the entire history of APS!"

I took the extreme step of flat-out refusing to accept the new referrals, causing the supervisor to turn his back and walk away in a huff. Good thing, too, because he was a lot bigger than me. I regretted my outburst almost immediately.

> *"What would yuh do if yuh saw a man drownin'?" duh guy says.*
> *"Do? Why, I'd jump in an' pull him out," I says. "Dat's what I'd do."*

The next morning, I came into the office early, dressed in a hair shirt, and profusely apologetic. Back then, refusing a supervisor's order was almost as unthinkable as telling off a drill sergeant.

I took on all the new referrals.

Nevertheless, the mere fact that I would feel compelled to speak this way to a supervisor told me I had reached my breaking point. It was that inter-office contretemps that truly signaled the end of my tenure at

Adult Protective Services, even if it took several more weeks for me to give formal notice.

I have never in my life been so comfortable with a decision.

And, as for the Goddam Borough of Brooklyn, I says, "ya know where ya can stick your geography."

Epilogue:
A Proclamation

In researching this book, I came upon an old novel about APS workers, based on "real life cases." The situations were real life, but the workers, the clients, and the settings were all made up, making this book close to a work of pure fiction.

I thought I still might pick up a few illuminating insights, although that didn't turn out to be the case. There were few, if any, stories in there that I hadn't experienced, and that weren't already explored in the book you've been reading. But then I got to the end of the novel.

In its final scene, the fictional county APS staff working the Christmas holiday was gathered in the big conference room in celebration of the New Year. There was a large Christmas tree adorned with globes and tinsel, garlands and greeting cards. There was a punch bowl and lots of sugary snacks. Everyone was standing around munching M&Ms and cookies, laughing, kidding each other and sharing their war stories. There were a few tears shed. In my experience, this scenario was more than a little on the hokey side. I've never known APS workers to get all soft and mushy around each other, at Christmas or any other time.

Anyway, the laughter and gaiety briefly ceased, as the APS workers welcomed their supervisor into their midst. He was, on balance, a decent fellow, but definitely not one of them. Then the supervisor got up and announced to the assembled partiers that the higher-ups in the social service organization had issued a proclamation, along with a plaque, that was now hanging in his office. In bold italics, it commemorated the members of the APS unit as the "Do Something Crew."

"A lot of times," the supervisor explained, "it doesn't matter what we do, as long as we respond, somehow...."

And that hit me, because, at its heart, that is what Adult Protective Services is all about. Although, I suppose, in a larger sense, it is what every social service organization that sends its workers out into the unknown is all about.

Many times, you can solve clients' problems, or at least make their difficult lives somewhat better, by the application of creativity, honest effort, and a lot of patience.

And many times, no matter how hard you try, and how much you care, you can't solve their problems and make anything appreciably better.

But what you can do—what you can *always* do—is show up, with a willingness to listen and bear witness to their stories, take risks and fully engage with people with whom in your private life you would never even dream of engaging on any level.

More often than any of us realize, just showing up makes a positive difference in the lives of our clients. Think of it from the client's perspective: a complete stranger has just walked into your home who genuinely cares about your problems and wants to help you. That sends a message of hope to almost anyone who may have never felt anything but hopeless, fearful, and completely alone in the world.

Every time an APS worker, anywhere in this country, walks through a door armed with that mentality, that worker has already made himself or herself worthy of a commemorative plaque.

And Heaven forfend, maybe even a raise.

Index

Index